CW00348057

Running Your Own

·S·H·O·P·

Running Your Own

S·H·O·P

Second Edition

Roger Cox

First published in Great Britain in 1985
by Kogan Page Limited, 120 Pentonville Road, London N1 9JN

Second edition 1989, reprinted with revisions 1992

British Library Cataloguing in Publication Data
Cox, Roger
Running your own shop—2nd ed.
1. Great Britain. Shops. Management
I. Title
658.8'7'00941

ISBN 1-85091-773-6

Printed and bound in Great Britain by
Biddles Limited, Guildford

Contents

Acknowledgements
I should like to acknowledge, with many thanks, the help given to me by successful shopowners including Angela and Trevor Beer, Ian Cook and Ray Vamplew. Thanks are also due to the manager of my branch of the National Westminster Bank for help, particularly for advice on Chapter 5. A debt is due for many ideas from a NEDO series, now sadly out of print, including 'Gold in Your Hands', 'Space Age Retailer', 'From Facts to Fortunes' and 'Grow Your Own Sales Staff'.

Additionally, I must acknowledge Alan Fiber's invaluable work, *Complete Guide to Retail Management*, from which numerous checklists, paragraphs and ideas have contributed to this book and any identical material used in any edition of this book remains the copyright of Alan Fiber.

Roger Cox
January 1992

Chapter 1

Retailing and You

Retailing is one of those areas of knowledge which we are all familiar with. After all, many of us are buying or just looking around shops almost every day. This thought must persuade some would-be entrepreneurs that shopkeeping is easy, a 'soft option'; all you need is a pleasant manner and some experience of handling money and you're well on the way to becoming another Jack Cohen (the founder of Tesco). Simple shopkeeping is not easy and presents a substantial challenge, as this book shows.

We often hear or read about the 'retail revolution', but retailing does not change particularly fast—it evolves steadily, as do the mechanical design and styling of cars. But once in the industry, the shopkeeper has to be alert to change. The beauty of retailing is that it is very near to the cash register. The cash register shows how changes happen. They may be tiny—small changes in consumer tastes which over time can mean success or failure to the retailer. If you run a shop you have to be aware of these changes—and adapt to them. This book tells you how to start and how to finish—successfully.

How retailing is going

The number of shops in Britain is going down—fast. In 1971 the government's census of this sector showed that there were 504,781 retail outlets. A different but similar survey by the Department of Trade and Industry for 1988 showed that £115 billion-worth of goods was sold in 338,000 British shops. In other words, the number of shops in Britain has fallen by one-third in 17 years.

Turnover of large multiple outlets rose by 118 per cent between 1980 and 1988, says the 1991 edition of the *Business Monitor*, and that of single outlet (independent) retailers by 65 per cent. By 1988 the multiples accounted for about 61 per cent of all retail trade, as against just 40 per cent in 1976. The retail trades showing most growth between 1980 and 1988 were alcoholic drink, confectionery and tobacco. Of the non-food retailers those that did well were, particularly, chemists, booksellers and photographic goods retailers.

The reasons usually adduced for the rise of the multiple (normally defined as a shop organisation with more than 10 branches) in recent years are:

1. The redevelopment of existing shopping centres to provide bigger shops with better facilities at, inevitably, higher rents which existing independent shopkeepers may find prohibitive.
2. Other costs, such as wages and rates, have risen disproportionately because of the reduction in central government support grants to local authorities and general wage pressure by unions.
3. Multiple companies and cooperative societies are rationalising their chains, closing down smaller units and opening fewer, larger ones.
4. Competition from multiples with their bigger shops, better buying terms and greater market penetration through more shops, and keen prices, is making it increasingly difficult for smaller, independent shops to stay in business.

That is the bad side. On the other hand, many independent retailers have found a niche in their particular markets which has made them to some extent immune to the competition from the big battalions. The secret lies in either location or specialisation and lots of hard work. Some smaller shops can survive because they are sited away from competition. Remember, if the big multiple companies are closing down their smaller shops in some towns, this gives a chance for the smaller operator.

Similarly, big multiples are reducing their product ranges to the best sellers, the brand leaders, and even cutting out whole ranges of goods. This gives an entry to shops which can fill the gaps with goods that people still want. Many small shops keep open longer hours than big shops thus providing more convenience to shoppers—another attraction. Shoppers often forget certain items when they do their main shop and the local retailer benefits from this 'top-up' shopping. Remember, too, that 40 per cent of British families still do not own cars and this may reduce their trips to big superstores. By looking at your local town—or some other area which you might investigate—you can see what is needed, what is lacking.

This is what marketing is about—identifying consumer needs and satisfying them in a mutually beneficial way, ie so that you make a profit and customers (in sufficient numbers) are satisfied. But if you are to go it alone you need to check out your strengths and weaknesses as a person. You need a self-assessment.

Self-assessment

Going it alone is a daunting thing for many people and it is worth while sitting down before you commit yourself to anything and trying to assess yourself honestly. A checklist of points follows and, even if you don't quite measure up to all of them, at least you'll have a better knowledge of your own strengths and weaknesses and can adjust and improve accordingly. Either way, find someone who knows you really well and is prepared to give a candid assessment; this will act as a good check on your own views of yourself. Ten to one the two of you won't agree on everything, but the exercise will help your self-knowledge no end. The checklist:

1. I am a self-disciplined and decisive person.
2. I am prepared for really hard work at all times and will ignore diversions such as the pub or TV.
3. I have the full support of my family.
4. I get on well with all types of people.
5. I have the drive to operate under stress and keep on until I have achieved the task.
6. I listen to advice.
7. I have good health.

You must be able to answer 'yes' to the majority of these questions; otherwise self-employment in the retail industry is not for you. Please stop reading now if you don't think you're up to this challenge.

Chapter 2

More Questions, More Ideas

You may not have any clear idea at this point of what exactly you want to do in the retail industry. For example, what sort of retail trade had you in mind? Where do you want to open your shop? Do you want to start afresh or buy into an existing business? What sort of legal structure were you thinking of for your business? We now try to answer some of these questions or at least to offer a range of alternatives.

Choosing a retail trade

The retail industry is made up of many different 'trades'—an old word referring to the processing through which materials had to go in the shop before they were sold. For example, the tailor would measure you for a suit and then make it up for you; the grocer filled up pound bags of sugar from a big wooden sugar barrel; the toymaker carved his own toys, and so on. Today with the advent of pre-packaging and ready-mades, the retailer normally displays the products for sale only after buying them from a manufacturer or wholesaler. But it is possible to get ideas on what trade to choose from a number of sources.

- Perhaps you have a hobby or qualification you enjoyed acquiring. Maybe you are interested in computers or cycling. How about a shop selling computers, or cycles, or DIY equipment or . . . ?
- Previous work experience: Trevor Beer was a senior buyer in a well-known department store chain. He and his wife, Angela, now run a successful high-class womenswear shop in Cheshire. In some cases you might have to take legal advice about competing against former employers.
- Acquiring some experience in the retail area by working for someone else on a full- or part-time basis. This need only be for a few weeks and it is surprising how happy some retailers are to take on this sort of help (paid or

unpaid!) even though they realise that you may become a competitor.

- A walk down your local high street will identify any gaps in the market or weaknesses among existing retailers where you may be able to compete effectively. Some trades such as fishmongering are dying out fast so that even large towns no longer have wet fish shops; new food trades such as delicatessen are springing up to match the needs of large numbers of people who have developed tastes for more off-beat foods due to their holidays abroad.

The most popular retail trades for the newly self-employed seem to be small general shops and CTNs (confectioner-tobacconist-newsagent). The general shop often sells a mixture of pre-packaged foodstuffs and various household items (like the typical village shop discussed on page 23).

The food trades—butchery, bakery and greengrocery—need some specialised knowledge because you will probably be expected to butcher meat or bake bread on your own premises. Greengrocery is less demanding in terms of knowledge, but the range of fruit and vegetables demanded by shoppers, particularly in the south east, continues to widen. Basically, if you want to feel safe in food retailing you should concentrate on pre-packaged products supplied by reputable manufacturers. Note the growing trend in Britain towards American style 'convenience stores'. These are bright, well designed shops—similar to fast food outlets—which offer extended shopping hours and efficient service. The merchandise on offer combines basic foodstuffs, household items, snack foods, hot, cold and alcoholic drinks, with newspapers, cigarettes and video hire as well. If you are thinking of going into the drinks trade as an off-licence owner, you will need to apply for and secure a licence from magistrates at the local Brewster Sessions. These licences are much easier to get today than they were before the big movement of the multiples, including supermarkets, into this trade.

For CTNs you have to make sure that you have a wholesaler who will supply you with papers in your area. Most wholesalers will not supply new paper shops—only those which are established—unless there is no competition.

Chemists' shops in Britain must have a qualified pharmacist on the premises to dispense ethical pharmaceutical products, ie drugs subject to legal control. A separate pharmacy for making up medicines must also be provided.

Quite a lot of women seem to fancy setting up boutiques and many have been hugely successful. But this is a fast changing market and even if you get it right locally and build up your custom, fashion alters so quickly today that you can often be caught wrong-footed. See, for instance, the boom in chains like Next, Benetton and Anonymous and the recent revolution in female late-teen wear. To some extent, the same arguments apply to menswear and childrenswear.

Household goods such as furnishings, electrical products, ironmongering and so on are now sold very much on brand manufacturers' advertised names, eg Hotpoint, but the independent retailer must watch the encroachment of multiple chains on these preserves. A monster called the Large Mixed Retailer (LMR) has emerged over the past decade and this multiple stocks all the popular lines from several different trades. Examples of this new kind of big shop are Boots, WH Smith and Tesco superstores. The trend is for these shops, along with the specialists like MFI (furniture), Sainsbury-Homebase (DIY, garden products etc), Comet (electrical products) to locate in edge-of-town sites away from conventional shops. You can often see two or three different specialist and LMR stores together at a big road junction. Even Marks & Spencer have publicly declared that they are now looking at this kind of edge-of-town site. The presence or the development of such big stores, turning over up to £20 million a year, can decimate the local shop population if they offer similar products at much lower prices. The lesson is clear. It is worth a check in the local authority planning department to see whether there are any plans for such developments. Forewarned is forearmed.

People with a real sense of marketing see themselves as problem-solvers. We all need feeding and clothing. Once we have houses we need to furnish them and so on. Human wants, the economists tell us, are endless. The retailer has a big role to play here in supplying them in a convenient way. Nowhere is this more true than with services such as hairdressing, dry cleaning and repairs of various kinds. One way of entering this area of retailing is through franchising (discussed on pages 21-2). Some retailers do not even have shops as such; they have mobile shops or market stalls, do door-to-door or party selling, use vending machines and so forth. The scope of this book does not extend to these peripheral areas of retailing and neither does it discuss the providing of services except in the context of franchising.

Buying existing businesses

Unless you are an expert in a particular trade, or in retailing generally, it is probably advisable not to start afresh unless you have access to really good advice. You will need to see accounts of the existing business for at least three years to work out the return on investment (net profit expressed as a percentage of the capital value of the business). Here again your advisers, such as your accountant and solicitor, are invaluable. One way of buying into an existing business is to take up a franchise.

Timing

In certain trades the timing of the start-up is important. In one case, a florist nearly failed when he opened his shop in the spring just as flowers were becoming plentiful in people's gardens. He realised he'd have done better starting in the autumn. The same is true of some other trades such as toys.

Location

Most retailers try to maximise their profit by maximising their turnover. Consequently, they tend to choose relatively accessible locations such as existing shopping centres. Location is the most critical factor for success in retailing and no decision can be made without collecting and analysing available information. You have to be sure that the population of your catchment area is large enough to support your shop. If you are taking over an existing business, the figures in the accounts of the business will tell their own story. Is the reason for selling that the owner can't build up his turnover because the local population is too small? The population may be large enough, but competition may be taking a large part of it away.

In a bigger shopping centre the number and quality of outlets is one of the most significant factors in a siting decision. But the bigger and better the centre the higher the rent and rates—although to gain real profitability, you should go (like the multiples) to big centres for high turnovers. Unfortunately, the multiples have a national name and you haven't.

According to most retail researchers, the degree of accessibility of a shopping centre is of prime importance. By accessibility is meant nearness to heavy pedestrian flows, generated by other shops or by bus stations, car parks and so on.

You should, therefore, gather information about the size of the local population, the kind of people living in the area and likely to use your shop, the size of the shopping centre and its general accessibility. You should visit the planning department of the local authority responsible for the area. The planning authority may intend deliberately to alter the shopping environments by imposing parking restrictions, building car parks, making pedestrianised streets and allowing developers to build new shops, quite apart from encouraging or discouraging people to settle in an area. You should keep an eye on the Register of Planning Applications, council minutes and the local press.

The catchment area of a shopping centre is the geographical area from which it draws its custom, that is, its total market. There can, of course, be no hard and fast line dividing the area of influence of one centre from another, but the main factors influencing catchment area size and shape may be summarised as:

1. Business attractions of a shopping centre consisting of:
   (a) types of major stores such as department stores which act as 'magnets';
   (b) kinds and selection of merchandise and services offered;
   (c) delivery, credit and other retail services;
   (d) reputation of major retailers;
   (e) banking facilities;
   (f) car parking, bus routes and other transport facilities, including the degree of restriction on cars.
2. Social and amusement attractions.
3. Population of area.
4. Density of population.
5. Class of consumer.
6. Resistance to travel and local 'psychology of distance'. (In the London area people seem to be prepared to drive longer distances to shop than in other parts.)
7. Lines of communication, consisting of:
   (a) local newspaper circulation area, sales and readership;
   (b) local radio coverage.
8. Car ownership in the market.
9. Nature of competition offered by other shopping centres within or near the market.
10. Topography of market area, including trunk roads, hills, rivers etc shielding or cutting off market area sections.

It is useful to purchase a large scale plan of the area. A company called Charles Goad Ltd publishes plans showing the position of all shops in a shopping centre, showing their names, addresses, trades and relative sizes. Count the number of pedestrians at various sections of the shopping centre at different times of the day and week. These figures of shopper density should be marked off on the map.

There is of course a strong connection between the density of shopper flows and the siting of well-known multiple shops like Marks & Spencer. Rent and rates, however, tend to be very high in these so-called 'primary' locations. Secondary and tertiary positions in a shopping centre are certainly less expensive and likely to be occupied by smaller multiples, independently owned shops and some service trades. On the other hand, pedestrian flows fall off progressively as the trading strength of retailers diminishes.

The important factors to be considered in connection with actual locations are:

1. Cumulative attraction or 'pull' of the centre, that is the number of shop units of all kinds and their quality (for example, the proportion of multiple shops).
2. Compatibility: the amount of spin-off sales which are generated by other 'sympathetic' trades—possibly service trades such as banks, building societies and so on.
3. Competitive strengths—the number of other shops competing with you.
4. Accessibility of potential site to the main shopping centre, particularly with regard to the position of 'magnets' such as Marks & Spencer, department stores and the like. The strength of business interception should be assessed, eg the site may or may not be located between a bus station or car park and the major multiples thus giving the benefit of passing trade. The shop's accessibility from the main entry points to the shopping centre is also important, along with parking facilities and restrictions, public transport frequency, and siting of bus stops.
5. Factors inherent at the site itself such as size, corner position and so on.

It is extremely difficult to make assessments of potential sales, particularly if you are considering opening a completely new business on a site. This is where some knowledge of a shop in your chosen trade is of great use because you can compare your site with an existing shop. A good starter is to estimate all your potential overheads, including a reasonable salary for yourself, a return on capital employed (say 15 per cent) and gross it up based on the mark-ups shown on page 35. This will show how much you will have to take in sales to be successful. Does the site look as though it could make it?

An example:

	£
Total overheads including a salary for yourself	20,000
Return on investment (say 20% on £40,000 capital)	8,000
	28,000

Profit margin 20 per cent (mark-up of 25 per cent, see page 35).

Total annual sales required £28,000 x 5=£140,000.

Training for shop owners

Many polytechnics, colleges and business schools have developed short (6 to 10 week) courses to advise people on how to start their own businesses. At Thames Polytechnic, for example, 25 per cent of the entrants to the course are would-be shop owners. Such courses deal with raising finance, taxation, finding a market and choosing premises. Participants are usually assisted in drawing up their own business plans and often speak highly of the design and expertise of these courses. The government helps to fund many of these developments which are much more widespread than is usually thought. Many local authorities now run their own courses for entrepreneurs who are willing to set up small businesses within the authority boundaries.

Structure of your business

There are basically three legal structures which you can adopt for the organisation and recognition of your business: sole trader, partnership or private limited company.

Sole trader

This is the easiest kind of business to set up and means that you are the person who is completely responsible for the conduct of the business, notably, that you are personally liable for all its debts. There are no special legal formalities and you can start trading whenever you like. You will be liable for income tax as a self-employed person and, although it is desirable, your accounts needn't be audited professionally. You will be liable also for VAT if your business turns over £35,000 or more a year (1991-2 figure); this should, of course, be immediately.

Partnership

A partnership occurs when two or more people are in business together. It is just as easy to set up a partnership as a sole trader business and the advantages are that the financial and working load is shared. Like the sole trader, each partner is personally liable for all the firm's business debts. This means that you may have to pay debts incurred without your knowledge by a fellow partner. This 'unlimited liability' idea can mean creditors securing a court order to seize personal effects to cover their unpaid bills. It goes without saying that people in partnership should trust each other absolutely.

Furthermore, disputes may occur within partnerships even with the mutual trust of friends. A verbal agreement on partnership is not enough and it's better to have a formal partnership agreement legally drawn up to avoid problems. Problems which could arise include profit splits, functional responsibilities, how to value members' assets on the death or departure of a partner and so on.

Private limited company

Once you set up an incorporated business, as a company is called, then you are protected from personal bankruptcy, unlike sole traders and partners. This limited liability is created by the fact that a company is a legal entity which exists quite separately from its founder and shareholders.

The company must have at least one director and a company secretary. As a director you are not the owner of the business—you are an employee. In this case your salary is taxed on Schedule E (PAYE). Companies are quite strictly controlled under the Companies Acts and company accounts must be audited annually by a qualified accountant. You therefore need advice from not only a qualified accountant but also a solicitor—you cannot start trading until you have received your Certificate of Incorporation from the Registrar of Companies and you will need advice on filling in two documents, the Memorandum and Articles of Association, which form part of your application to become a company. You can, however, buy an existing company off-the-shelf from a company broker if you are in a hurry.

Business names

You may trade under your own name or under the name of the shop: 'The Dairy', for example. Whatever you decide, you must disclose your own name (and any partners' names) and address on all business forms, and display it in the shop. This shows where documents can be served if necessary. The Companies Act 1981 stipulates this not only for companies but for all unincorporated businesses, like sole traders. When picking a name a useful booklet to read is *Business Names—Guidance Notes* published by the Department of Trade and Industry.

Premises

Many questions arise in connection with the shop unit you are looking for. The most important factor in retailing is location, ie how many 'chimney pots' are there around your shop? How accessible is your shop to its market and is there a good passing trade? The answers to these questions depend to some extent on the trade you have chosen to be in, but getting the right answers is vital to you (they are contained in *Buying a Shop*, published by Kogan Page).

Is the shop suitable for what you have in mind? Is it a good size? A modern standard shop unit has around a 16-foot frontage to the street and a full depth of maybe 80 feet which would include space for storage, office and so on. Some older shops have arcaded entrances. Ian Cook took over an old shoe shop in South London and converted it into a DIY outlet but he had to take out the arcade and remodel the front to gain extra sales space.

Do you intend to live 'over the shop' if there is appropriate accommodation? Trevor Beer and his wife sold up their four-bedroomed detached house to help finance their purchase of a shop in Cheshire with accommodation above it; they lived in it for two years before moving back into a house similar to the one they had previously sold. It is clearly cheaper to do this and it does improve the security of stock, especially if you have direct access to the shop floor from the flat or maisonette.

The procedures for buying or renting a shop are very similar to those which almost all of us have been through in connection with domestic housing. Although there are now a number of books on conveyancing and buying your own house, it would be wise to consult your legal adviser in the case of shop property. Your solicitor will be able to check whether you are in line with the occasionally complicated regulations governing business premises. For example, there could be a clause in your lease or property deeds which forbids or restricts certain business activities. This is particularly common in retailing. A multiple retailer vacating one shop and moving into larger premises nearby can stipulate that the succeeding tenant may not carry on the same trade as the multiple.

There may be lease clauses which affect assignment and subletting rights, rights to change the use, and rights to make alterations, additions and improvements. In addition, length of lease, review clauses, repairing and insurance obligations, service charges (as in managed shopping centres), the rent-free period for shopfitting and so forth should be examined. Again there may be local bylaws which restrict your trade. You may have to apply for planning permission even though you may own the freehold of the property. This requires the submission of all plans for acceptance by the local authority involved, including shopfronts and fascias, external signs, car parking and so on. Shopfitters should be able to give help in the actual production of plans for submission. Particularly if you are buying the property you will need a report on its fabric from a building surveyor who will tell you what repairs, if any, are required; and this report may be a useful bargaining counter when you negotiate a price. It will also enable you to start off with a clean sheet on a programme of maintenance.

Franchising

An increasingly popular alternative to setting up your own shop 'cold' is to buy a franchise. According to the Power Survey, franchised sales in 1990 exceeded £5.24 billion, an increase of 11 per cent on the 1989 figure. Over 350 companies offer business format franchises in the UK.

Franchising, by definition, is where a company (the franchisor) establishes a contractual relationship with owners of separate businesses—franchisees—which operate under the franchisors' names in a specified manner and in a given geographical area, to market the product or service.

Many of us associate franchises with fast-food retailing, but the range of franchised products and services which can be sold from shop premises is very much wider. It includes bridal attire, footwear, kitchen equipment, motor and cycle accessories, DIY products, computers, health foods, confectionery, dry cleaning, photo-processing, keep-fit and many others. The retail voluntary groups discussed in Chapter 7 are also a kind of franchising.

Running a franchise can be less risky than going into business in the normal do-it-yourself way. Whereas the usual business venture may be a step into the unknown, a franchise is often a tried and tested operation. But franchises are not an automatic passport to a fortune: they require hard, sustained work on the part of the franchisee and, occasionally, they throw up the unscrupulous franchisor who tries to exploit inexperienced people who have money to invest in a business venture.

Each franchisee should insist on a full disclosure being made of the manner in which the franchisor proposes to charge his franchise fee, for there are ways of disguising the charge. For the use of their name and trading style, franchisors may charge anything from £2500 to over £75,000 but usually this expense is in the £30,000-plus range (in 1991). Additionally, the franchisee will need money for premises and equipment, along with working capital. The franchisor may then charge a continuing fee, as a straight royalty, a percentage on gross sales, or through the compulsory purchase of goods by the franchisee from either the franchisor or a nominated supplier of the franchisor.

It is clear, then, that franchisees have to produce two profits—one for the franchisee and one for the franchisor. Few businesses can do that easily these days and you may come to resent what you see as your hard-earned profits being taken away.

Balancing the costs, the franchisee receives a number of benefits, notably the training that should be given by the franchisor company to enable the franchise to be run properly, free help and advice, and the support of the franchisor's natural advertising and promotional activities.

Before signing a franchise contract, there are a number of questions which should be asked of the franchisor:

1. How long have you been franchising?
2. How many failures have you had?
3. May I have a copy of your contract?
4. What happens if I wish to end the contract?
5. Are you a member of the British Franchising Association?

The BFA is the ethical and regulatory body for British franchising and is designed to cut out the 'cowboys'; about a third of British franchisors are BFA members. No contract should be signed without the advice of your solicitor or accountant. There are other areas about which questions should be asked and you are referred to the many excellent reference books on the subject including *Taking up a Franchise* and *The Good Franchise Guide*, also published by Kogan Page.

The village shop

Those of us who live in towns may well have been attracted to the idea of running a village shop—perhaps as a second best alternative to being landlord of the village pub! The idea conjures up a picture of an idyllic existence: getting to know the salty village characters, mulching the roses in the garden of the little cottage you've bought near the shop.

The Rural Development Commission, a government-funded organisation, estimates that during the next five years at least half of the village shops in England will have been forced to close. The reasons? A huge increase in the costs of running such shops, a sharp fall in the numbers of agricultural workers and growing competition from multiple organisations. John White, a retail officer with the Rural Development Commission, says that an average village shop might expect to turn over around £60,000 a year. On this basis, and allowing for a profit margin of about 16 per cent, gross profit would be around £9600. Out of this will have to come rent or mortgage repayments, transport costs, pay for relief staff, rates, heating, lighting, telephone bills, plus other charges such as the cost of theft or advertising. This should leave the shopkeeper with net profits of about £200. (Beware, in this case, of 'raiding' the till—trading losses lie that way!) Costs of local authority rates, electricity and other services are high because they are connected with business premises, even though a large proportion may relate to living accommodation above or to the rear of the shop. The Rural Development Commission recognises the growing problems of retail shops and fields eight retail consultants around the country.

The people who used to patronise village shops have changed. There are fewer agricultural labourers but, particularly in the south, they have been partly replaced by the wealthy who have moved to homes in the country. Because these newer arrivals are mobile they may well shop in nearby towns at large multiple stores with parking space.

The changing pattern of rural life may look threatening, but it also offers the village shopkeeper an opportunity. Village stores must adapt if they are to survive.

The big advantage of the village shop is often its lack of close competition. Service and quality rather than price should be the keynote. As John White of the Rural Development Commission says, 'The delicatessen counter is a good way to compete with supermarkets. Products sold here often command better margins than basic lines which supermarkets, with their bulk-buying capacity, can sell more cheaply.' Local markets must be researched carefully by would-be village shopkeepers in order to avoid the problems of poor buying. In particular, it may be useful to look at extra sources of income to supplement a return which may be very low. Such alternatives include acting as a sub post office. John White tells of one village shopkeeper who started a successful second business curing bacon from local farms which he then sold to other village shopkeepers. Above all, the village shop owner must obtain and keep the goodwill of his customers and this means giving them what they want, when they want it. However you answer the questions you may ask yourself, if you decide to go into retailing, to succeed you must:

1. Choose a trade and location which offer a good chance of success.
2. Identify and get to know your customers and their wants.
3. Decide how you are going to appeal to them and draw them into your shop to buy.
4. Devise and implement a total shop identity which will create a successful image and appeal to your customers.

Chapter 3

Raising Capital

One of the most important things you have to do is to raise the money for the shop and its fittings, and stock. You will also need money for working capital, that is to pay the day-to-day expenses of the business. Ray Vamplew opened a bookshop in Lambeth and for the first year or so found customers few and far between. He had used only his own resources rather than supplementing them with a loan, and had to pay his shop running expenses without much of a cash flow from sales. Ray reckons that you should have your hands on more than enough cash to cover these outlays from the start.

Using your own money

It is always desirable to be able to show to the bank or any other lender that you have a financial stake in the business; that is, you're able to invest some of your own money in it. This money may come from a redundancy payment, a lump-sum retirement annuity or your savings. Take stock of your assets: securities, jewellery, antiques, vehicles and so forth. Many people take out second mortgages on their houses and this is particularly attractive today because house prices have, generally, risen by three or four times over the past 10 years.

Bank finance

A common source of cash is the bank which can offer a number of different kinds of financing. The most common form of bank finance is the overdraft. Although this is technically used to cover short-term cash flow difficulties (when money is going out but little is coming in) and to provide working capital, it can be renegotiated and 'rolled over' after the usual limit, one year. Banks recommend that if you need help for a one-off specific purpose, like buying a van, a short-term loan is more suitable. This may extend up to three years and your account is debited with equal repayment instalments each month.

Business development loans are also offered by banks and

these can be used to finance working capital or the purchase of property. The term of the loans can run up to 20 years and variable amounts of up to £250,000 may be available. It is vital that you prepare your request for funds carefully because your bank manager—or indeed any other lender—will be considering lending you other people's money of which he is the present custodian. Remember that large bank branches are able to lend more money than small local branches and that you should have introduced yourself to the branch manager before requesting a loan. The manager will invariably ask for some security or collateral against the loan and this might take the form of fixed assets in the business, stocks and shares and insurance policies, for example.

This is seen as providing proof of your commitment to the business. But some advisers suggest that you should not mortgage your house or other private possessions to support your business and that you should keep personal risks and business risks as separate as possible. You should, they advise, try to persuade people to lend you money on market grounds alone—on the likelihood of your project being a winner. If a bank insists, shop around; there will always be someone who will lend you the money more cheaply and for less collateral in what remains a buyer's market.

Small firms Loan Guarantee Scheme

If money is unavailable from the bank for any reason you may be eligible for a loan under the government Loan Guarantee Scheme. The government guarantees up to 70 per cent of the sum loaned by banks to small businesses; the maximum loan is £100,000. Borrowers pay a charge for the loan which is part interest payment to the lender and part guarantee premium to the government. Some banks act as lenders under the scheme and details are available at local branches.

The Rural Development Commission

If you are thinking of opening a village shop, the Rural Development Commission may be able to help. The Commission not only offers loans but also advice on the local economic situation along with professional consultancy and training services. Other regional bodies include the Scottish Development Agency and the Welsh Development Agency. You can also reach your local Small Firms Centre by telephoning freefone 'Enterprise direct' on 0800 222999 to be put through to your nearest Centre and see what advice they may be able to give.

Trade credit

Once you have started in business and have ordered stock you will most likely be allowed trade credit from your suppliers. By allowing you to pay over a period your supplier is, in effect, giving you a loan. This kind of loan does not carry interest as such, but you are offered a discount, usually around 2½ per cent, if you pay your invoice within, say, 30 days. Trade credit can often be very helpful to the small shopkeeper. Indeed, a supermarket owner who later became a multi-millionaire often did not pay his big name suppliers for six to eight months. Of course, he had his direct supplies cut off but he could still buy the same well-known brands from wholesalers and cash-and-carry warehouses. In a cash business he soon became very rich—but this method of becoming a millionaire is not recommended to shop owners!

How to convince the lender

Any lenders of capital have to be convinced that the business venture you hope to embark on will be a success. After all, they do want to see the loan paid back in the agreed fashion along with interest, because they are in business like yourself to make a profit. You are likely to go to your bank for finance and nothing impresses the bank manager more than a well thought-out case with all the relevant facts properly marshalled and clearly presented. The following information is likely to be required in a business proposal for a shop:

1. Name of proprietor(s), address and date.
2. Details of shop and its location.
3. Brief synopsis of personal details including age, education and experience.
4. Details of personal means, eg property, and other business connections.
5. For a type of business new to you, or a start-up situation, an outline of experience, ability and factors leading to your decision.
6. Details of premises, including dimensions, tenure and conditions, plans and surveyor's report.
7. If an existing retail business, when established,

purpose, how it has evolved, main factors contributing to progress, current reputation, past three years' audited accounts (if available) and current position, up-to-date balance sheet figures, eg debtors, creditors, stock, bank balance, borrowings, fixed assets (such as buildings, fixtures and fittings, machinery, vehicles).

8. The retail trade you wish to enter with a broad description of the kind of products or services you will sell, the selling methods and the type of customer you hope to attract.
9. Market research, including an assessment of spending on the products you will sell, the strength of competition, your own competitive advantages, eg quality, price competitiveness, location, and an estimate of annual sales, broken down on a month-by-month basis.
10. An estimate of gross profits per month from turnover and a detailed breakdown of operating costs to be set against them, culminating in a net profit projection.
11. A cash flow forecast, which will contain the same information as in 10, but showing the actual amounts during the months in which they are due to be paid; this should also show what is projected in the early part of the venture when outgoings may not be matched by income.
12. The amount of finance required and the purposes to which it will be put, showing when it will be needed. The amount should be enough to finance increased working capital requirements and contain a margin for unforeseen circumstances or for items which you may have forgotten to include in your costings. You will also need to stipulate the security you would be willing to put forward as security for the loan.

A spin-off from the not inconsiderable amount of work you will have to put in on producing a business plan is that you will be able to talk fluently and enthusiastically to the bank manager or any other lending institution you may approach, because you have done your homework.

Can we make a decent profit?

The sort of figures which you will need to convince not only the lender but yourself of the viability of the shop should be presented as shown on page 29. We've already seen in Chapter 2 how a typical village shop might perform and it's not a pretty sight.

The crunch question when considering a move into retailing should be, 'Is it worth keeping a shop?' This is where books of account can help but by the time these have been made up, it may be too late to say, 'No, it isn't!' It is therefore vital to try to answer this important question beforehand. We can do this on the basis of some simple figures.

First of all, you should have some sort of financial aim in mind. To work this out, think of what you might be making if you invested all your capital in a building society (maybe 10 per cent before tax, with reasonable security). At the same time you could be earning wages or a salary as an employee, assuming that there are suitable jobs available. The return on a small shop should be at least twice that amount (or 20 per cent) to cover you for all the risks involved in running a small business. That's on top of a fair salary for the actual work you do. To test this, let's assume that the net value or worth of your business including stocks and fittings is £60,000. The desirable minimum return at 20 per cent would then be £12,000, ie £60,000 x 20/100. Now £12,000 may seem quite a lot of money, even before tax. Let's assume that you are making this sort of return on your assets. What you're actually making might look like this:

	£
Net profit before paying yourself a salary	12,000
ADD	
Sales value of goods used by yourself	1,000
	13,000
LESS	
What you could earn elsewhere (average UK earnings)	10,000
Realistic profit	3,000

With a realistic profit way below the desirable minimum return you would be better off *financially* investing your money elsewhere. The same problem faces you whether you own the freehold of your shop or rent premises. We stress the word 'financially' as most people enter shopkeeping because it is a pleasant occupation and it provides self-employment.

Chapter 4

Keeping Track

Keeping the books in a business is often looked on as a bore. Some of us tend to avoid the things we dislike doing and small businesses put off doing the accounts often until the last minute. Then it is a rush to fill in the cash book, sort out the invoices, decipher the cheque book stubs and the rest. Running proper books of account is very necessary for the shop owner and in its importance is probably second only to buying. Accounts can tell you quickly what the financial position of the business is at any one time for control purposes, help you to forecast and plan for the future and provide the basis for the returns which you must make to the Inland Revenue and the VAT people. It's not, by the way, necessary for you to master accountancy; an accountant will prepare your final accounts and a balance sheet each year for you on the basis of the records you should keep.

There are two kinds of accounts in the well run business. Basic accounts tell us how the shop has performed over a stated period and are formed from the records which you should keep, as explained below. Management accounts, which use information from the basic accounts, tell you how the business is going so that improvements can be made and corrective action taken quickly.

Basic accounts

All transactions in the business should be recorded. The problem is, of course, finding the time to do it. There never seems to be spare time in a busy small business, especially if it is a new one. Quite a lot of people try to compromise; they keep their invoices, purchase orders, petty cash vouchers, wages records and petrol bills carefully in folders and hand the whole lot, along with their bank statements and cheque stubs, over to their accountant who then has to sort it out. This can be a very expensive way of keeping your accountant's Porsche going.

The five rules of good book-keeping are:

1. Keep only useful records.
2. Make records simple to use.
3. Be accurate—but not too accurate.
4. Guard against fraud.
5. Make records simple to *keep*.

Records kept in a business must be essential. You can become 'bogged down' with too much information and over-detailing and so you only need records which tell you something worth knowing about your business. Check with your accountant what information you really require. Basically you need six different sets of basic records to help you run your shop: a bank account; a cash book; a petty cash book; a wages record; a purchases record; a record of sales on credit.

These records are much easier to keep and use if they are on printed or duplicated forms (and not on the backs of envelopes!). In terms of accuracy, any calculations you make can be in round pounds. For your total annual sales, the nearest £100 will be accurate enough for most purposes. Obviously your cash books, customer records and so on must always be 100 per cent accurate. An efficient book-keeping system will discourage dishonesty among your staff and help reduce stock pilferage and cash theft.

A key document is the *cash book*. This is a badly named book, not to be confused with the petty cash book which records how cash is spent on small items such as postage stamps and window cleaning. The cash book is the business's own record of its bank statement. In choosing one for your shop, make sure that it has plenty of vertical columns. The more of these you have the more use it will be (see illustration on page 33). Generally, about twice as many columns for payments as for receipts are needed. Make a point of recording all your payments and receipts in your cash book. Value added tax should be noted separately and the totals of receipts and payments should be entered gross. Although the cash book, as we have said, is the shop owner's record of his or her business bank account, entries in it will almost always be different from the bank statement. This is because of delays in crediting cheques paid in and debiting cheques paid to creditors. At least once a month add up the cash book, cross-check with the bank statement, work out the balance and carry it forward as a receipt if in credit and as a payment if not.

Make cash payments out of your petty cash float and not straight out of the till so that your cash banked and your recorded sales agree. Treat your *petty cash book* as completely separate from your cash book. The petty cash itself should be kept in a cash box separate from the cash register. Experience will tell you how much the petty cash float should be (maybe £100). Record the float as a payment in your cash book and as a receipt in your petty cash book, remembering to include VAT. From time to time make up the float to its original total by 'claiming from' your cash book for exactly the amount spent from the float. This imprest system helps you check your petty cash float against the petty cash book.

Wages forms are produced in many excellent systems which use carbon or carbonless paper to provide you with a payroll record, the employee's payslip and the individual's pay record. Make sure that the wages you pay out, your net wages bill, agree with the entries in your cash book. Once a month check that PAYE, superannuation and National Insurance agree with the actual sum deducted from your employees, together with your own NI contributions.

Purchase records often give people trouble because much of the goods are supplied on credit. You can use purchase day books and purchase ledgers (rather like cash books) but a simpler method is to use a system of ordinary loose-leaf files and a calculator. As you receive your purchase invoices check that (a) you have received the goods, (b) that the prices are correct and (c) that they are calculated correctly. After checking, put them in a file marked 'Finances awaiting attention'. Clear this file once a week and add up the amount of each purchase invoice on your calculator. This total should be added to the balance on a 'Schedule of outstanding payments' and each invoice filed by the supplier's name.

When suppliers' statements of account arrive (these summarise the invoices already sent to you) they are a reminder that payment is usually due on all invoices 30 days old or more. Check the statements against unpaid invoices and deduct any discounts allowed for prompt payment. Make out a cheque and enter the cheque and discounts separately in your cash book. Mark the invoices as 'paid' and transfer them to a file marked 'Paid invoices', again filed by suppliers.

Finally, add together payments for purchases and discounts received as shown in your cash book and deduct the total from the balance outstanding in your 'Schedule of outstanding payments'. In this way, your schedule will always be up to date, give or take a few days.

A similar system can be used for credit sales. In this way you

Expenses side of the cash book

Date	*Total*	*Purchases*	*Wages*	*Services**	*Insurance*	*Maintenance*	*Miscel-laneous*	*Petty cash*	*VAT*	*Bank*	*Repayments and interest*
	£	£	£	£	£	£	£	£	£	£	£
1.3.85	389.77	201.21	6.47	115.40	—	—	—	4.90	29.63	32.16	—
4.3.85	599.97	463.80	18.91	—	—	16.00	8.38	1.53	41.39	49.96	—
5.3.85	806.58	355.40	—	—	40.00	—	—	—	36.75	24.43	350.00

**May be broken down into telephone, electricity, water etc.*

can—if you must offer credit—operate a simple credit control system in which you can analyse your debtors.

Talk of control and analysis brings us on to the second kind of accounts we previously mentioned—management accounts.

Management accounts

What the basic accounts tell us is how the shop has performed over the past period: its history. These accounts and their key elements, the cash book, are a poor indicator of a business's health. You might look at the cash balance you have in your cash book and interpret it as the money in your till at the end of the day, plus your bank balances. There are four reasons why the cash balance is a misleading figure for control:

1. If you allow credit you may not be paid for goods until long after you've sold them. Customers have been known to take up to a year to pay.
2. You pay for some goods before you sell them; for others, after.
3. Long-term expenses, such as rates, often have to come out of what looks like a healthy cash balance.
4. You need different amounts of money tied up in stock at different times of the year.

The really reliable way to see how well you are doing is to keep management accounts which show your gross profit and your expenses or overheads. Net profit, the figure which counts as your return on your investment, is the difference between the two:

Net profit=Gross profit−Overheads
(plus discounts from suppliers).

Let us now look at pricing in your shop.

Pricing for profit

Gross profit is what is left from your sales turnover after you have paid your suppliers of goods for resale. It is very often expressed as a percentage of sales. Then it is called the gross profit margin, ie:

$$\frac{\text{Gross profit}}{\text{Sales}} \times \frac{100}{1} \quad \text{or} \quad \frac{\pounds 25{,}000}{100{,}000} \times \frac{100}{1} = 25\%$$

Shopkeepers are concerned with the gross margin on individual lines where the profit is expressed as a percentage of the selling price. The gross *mark-up* is the same profit expressed as a percentage of the *buying* price. For example, the mark-up percentage or

$$\frac{\text{Mark-up}}{\text{Cost Price}} \times \frac{100}{1} \text{ could be } \frac{5}{20} \times \frac{100}{1} = 25\%$$

Expressed as a percentage of the selling price or margin percentage we have:

$$\frac{\text{Margin}}{\text{Selling Price}} \times \frac{100}{1} = \frac{5}{25} \times \frac{100}{1} = 20\%$$

This table compares mark-ups and margins:

Mark-up %		*Margin* %
25	=	20
33⅓	=	25
50	=	33⅓
100	=	50

There is a list of mark-ups in many retail trades on page 113.

What we have just described is the *planned* gross profit in both mark-up and margin terms. Unfortunately, these make no allowances for breakages, pilferage, discounts to your staff or customers, mark-down and so on. In other words, these percentages are what you make in theory and so you ought to plan for a realised gross profit.

Cost of goods sold is an important determinant of the gross profit. This is the buying price value of the goods actually resold and is by far the biggest expense in goods (but not service) retailing. Here is an example of a simple trading account showing cost of goods sold:

	£	£
Sales		6,000
Opening stock value	1,000	
ADD Purchases	5,000	
	6,000	
LESS Closing stock value	2,000	
Cost of goods sold	4,000	
Gross profit	2,000	
	6,000	6,000

In order to make this calculation we have to know the value of our stocks at the beginning and at the end of the period; and how much we spent on purchases, ie Opening Stock+Purchases−Closing stock=Cost of goods actually sold; by taking this cost of goods value from our sales we can work out our net profit.

Cost of goods sold should also include broken, lost or stolen goods, trade and quantity discounts, carriage inwards and alteration or workroom costs (as in textiles).

Coming back to the price we charge for our merchandise, the ideal one should meet these requirements:

1. Sell the item within the average period of stock-room time.
2. Foster goodwill and encourage repeat trade.
3. Cover the buying price of the item, all selling and administration expenses connected with it, and produce a desired net profit.
4. Be in line with your own sales policies which could include the achievement of manufacturer's recommended price, or recognised trade list price (eg, *The Grocer* price-list) or meet competitors' prices.

Checking your gross profit

We said before that you should have some sort of early warning system to tell you how well—or how badly—you and your shop are doing. The two important figures to check are gross profit and expenses. Let's look at some ways in which you can check gross profit. We have already seen how gross profit is worked out in theory: recorded sales are taken for the period and from it are deducted the cost of the goods sold and of stock losses, breakages, discounts and so on. In practice it is rather more complicated and you should ask your accountant's advice on which of the three methods you should use.

Unit stock control method

This is the simplest method but it can only be used properly for bulky or expensive items such as electrical appliances, jewellery or fashion wear. With goods like these you can attach a ticket to each one, in code, to show its original cost. As you sell each item you take off the ticket and record, alongside the cost price, the price you received for it. 'Swing' tickets, such as the Kimball tag, can be purchased for such a system. At the end of, say, a month, you check your sales and receipts against the goods you have in stock. If you find anything missing this should be included in your cost of sales figure. For example:

	£	£
Month's recorded sales		4,000
LESS Cost of goods sold	2,000	
LESS Stock losses	200	2,200
Gross profit		1,800

As a percentage: $\frac{1800}{4000} \times \frac{100}{1} = 45\%$

Cost price method

This method is often used in retail trades which have a quick turnover of stock such as greengrocery. It involves counting and valuing your stock at *cost prices*. This means that you will have to file your invoices systematically to find the cost of goods in stock without too much trouble. One drawback is that the method cannot tell you what your *realised* gross margin is because it cannot reveal your stock losses. But so long as you use this method of calculating planned or theoretical gross margins on a consistent basis, the method is an excellent trend spotter. For example:

	£	£
Three months' sales		20,000
Opening stock at cost	1,000	
ADD Purchases at cost	15,000	
	16,000	
LESS Closing stock at cost	2,000	
Cost of goods sold	14,000	
Gross profit	6,000	
	20,000	20,000

As a percentage: $\frac{6,000}{20,000} \times \frac{100}{1} = 30\%$

Selling price method

This approach is used in trades where there is a large assortment of stock which is difficult to control. Do-it-yourself shops are a good example. Although the selling price method is not quite as accurate as the other two it does have three big advantages:

1. It gives you a pointer to both high and low gross profit lines as you go through all your purchase invoices and put a sales value on each.
2. It is a good indicator of how serious your unrecorded stock losses are (eg, from pilferage) because the *known* stock losses such as breakages can be built into your calculation.
3. It allows an interim (in-between) gross profit percentage to be estimated without taking a physical stock count.

This method is less accurate than the others because it takes an average based on retail selling prices and buying prices over a period (say a month). An example of a margin calculation using this method is as follows:

June: stock summary

	Cost prices £	*Margin* £	*Selling prices* £	*Margin* %
Opening stock 1 June	30,000	10,000	40,000	
Month's purchases	15,000	4,800	19,800	
Stock and month's purchases	45,000	14,800	59,800	24.7

Margin = Selling prices − cost prices
= 59,800 − 45,000
= £14,800

$$\text{Average margin} = \frac{\text{Margin x 100}}{\text{Sales}}$$

$$= \frac{14{,}800 \times 100}{59{,}800}$$

$$= 24.7\%$$

Now in order to calculate the gross profit more accurately, we adjust recorded sales by known losses and add in a percentage for pilferage (unknown losses). You can do this calculation each month until you feel the need for a complete stock count. In doing the gross profit calculation we have worked out 'sales plus adjustments' at both selling (£18,000) and cost (£14,160) price. We can then transfer these figures to the stock summary and deduct them from the opening stock plus the month's purchases to give us estimated stock values.

June: gross profit calculation

	£
Recorded sales	17,500
ADD Breakages at selling price	150
ADD Mark downs (reductions in price)	500
ADD Discounts to customers	130
ADD Stock loss provision (at 3% of sales)	520
Recorded sales and adjustments	18,800
LESS Average margin (24.7%)	4,640
Estimated cost of sales and adjustments	14,160
Recorded sales	17,500
Gross profit before stock count	3,340

$$\text{Gross profit as a percentage of Sales} = \frac{3{,}340}{17{,}500} \times \frac{100}{1} = 19.1\%$$

June: stock summary
(see previous stock summary table)

	Cost prices £	*Margin* £	*Selling prices* £
Stock and month's purchases	45,000	14,800	59,800
LESS Sales and adjustments	14,160	4,640	18,800
Estimated stock 1 July	30,840	10,160	41,000

By doing this on a monthly basis you will be able to see how gross profit percentages can be affected, over a period, by high breakage and mark-down rates. Also, by working out the margin percentages for each month's purchases you will be able to see how profitably you are buying. When we take stock we are able to check the estimated stock levels against the actual. This will show the true unknown stock loss and upon this, the estimated percentage put into our calculations (in the example, 3 per cent), can be made more accurate. Sometimes the stock loss provision may be overestimated, giving us a surplus on stock when physically counted. In this case the surplus stock value should be added back on to the last estimated stock figure before the physical count. Because the estimated stock value is

Budget forecast

	Feb £	*Mar* £	*Apr* £	*May* £	*Jun* £	*Jul* £
INCOME						
Cash sales	2,000	2,600	3,100	3,300	3,300	2,700
Credit sales	500	500	300	500	700	500
TOTAL INCOME	2,500	3,100	3,400	3,800	4,000	3,200
EXPENDITURE						
Stock purchases	2,000	2,500	3,000	2,750	2,500	2,250
GROSS PROFIT	500	600	400	1,050	1,500	950
OPERATING COSTS						
GWEP (gas, water, electricity, telephone)	60	60	60	60	60	60
Rates	90	90	90	90	90	90
Insurance	30	30	30	30	30	30
Cleaning and maintenance	20	20	20	20	20	20
Travel and motor	40	40	40	40	40	40
Advertising	10	10	10	10	10	10
Bank charges	10	10	10	10	10	10
Other expenses	10	10	10	10	10	10
VAT	70	80	60	140	70	120
TOTAL	340	350	330	410	340	390
NET PROFIT	160	250	70	640	1,160	560

the sum of the cost value and the margin, then both these latter figures will also be adjusted.

Quick gross profit check

If time is pressing there is a speedy method of calculating a rough estimate of gross profit. This is done by applying your estimated gross profit—based on last year's results and recent trends—to your actual sales over, say, a month or a quarter. A danger in this method is that actual gross profit can change quickly, especially if you start selling goods with different mark-ups from before. The only way to be as accurate as possible is to take stock and make the calculations already described.

Overhead costs

Gross profit is what we have left from sales revenues after paying for our merchandise. Out of this profit we have to pay expenses like rent and wages and, hopefully, at the end of the day we have our net profit left.

A simple budget statement will cover the planning and control of these expenses. Such a statement should give the name of the expense under main headings like 'Accommodation costs', 'Administration costs' and so on and should show last year's actual expense along with a forecast or budgeted figure for this year. Much finer control can be achieved by breaking the budgets down into quarters because many expenses are charged on a three-monthly basis. An example of such a budget is given on page 40.

In setting out the expense budget you should be careful to include only expenses that are due in a particular quarter, not the payments you make. For example, you pay your rates half-yearly. In the quarterly budget statement you should split the rates into two equal parts and enter them as costs whether you have paid them or not.

The budgeted expenses should then be compared with the actual expenses when the bills come in and any differences investigated. The extra costs may be outside your control, eg a rise in telephone charges, and you should amend your budgets for the rest of the year to reflect this charge.

Chapter 5

Employing People

Once a business grows beyond a certain size it is almost impossible to avoid employing someone from outside your own family.

Choosing good staff and using them effectively is probably the most difficult short-term problem in business—the problem of being an employer rather than being an employee.

It's not only because people are so different that they sometimes find difficulty in working harmoniously together. A great deal of legislation protecting the rights of employees has come out of Parliament during the past 20 or so years. Some of it may affect you, even in a small shop.

Choosing staff

The first thing to be worked out is what you want the proposed new member of staff to do. Jobs in retailing include working a cash register, price marking merchandise, checking merchandise against invoice, filling shelves or racks, personal selling to customers and other more mundane tasks.

Once you have decided this—and a new recruit may be expected to do several of these tasks—then you can decide what kind of person you need. Part-timers are very important in retailing and you may consider them for peak trading period coverage. First of all you need to describe the tasks clearly for yourself and to specify the experience, qualifications and temperament (pleasant, engaging personality, willingness to learn, and so on) of the person you need to do them. You also need to decide how much you are going to pay in wages. The difference between recruitment and selection has been described as attracting, first, the people who want to work with you and choosing, second, from among those the people you want to work with.

You will probably need to advertise the job first. This does not necessarily mean using a newspaper. A poster in your window will help. Any advertisement should state clearly what you are looking for. When you have sorted out the replies you can carry out interviews and make your selection from the people who present themselves. The interview is important in that it allows you to compare the applicants with the job description. Interviews should be conducted as far as possible in a quiet office and in a reasonably informal manner; the candidates tend to say more about themselves when relaxed. You should have studied what the applicant's letter has said and written down the questions you want to ask. Try to frame questions which allow open-ended answers; this means using the words 'how' and 'why' a lot and the answers to them will give clues to the experience and motivation of candidates. Remember that, even in these hard times, an interview is a two-way street. The candidate may not want your job and needs to be 'sold' it to some extent by receiving information about it and the firm in a positive way.

Checklist of assessment at the interview

1. Are they smart and presentable?
2. Do they have the experience and skills to do the job?
3. How well have they done in previous jobs?
4. If they lack skills, how motivated would they be to learn?
5. Do they have a positive attitude to other people and to their job?
6. What makes them tick?
7. Do they seem honest?
8. What references are available?

The interview should be done systematically, using the description of the job and comparing it with the strengths and weaknesses that you should tease out of the applicants. As to references, these are often best taken up on the telephone. Previous employers are more relaxed about what they say when there is no written record; watch out for hesitations over the phone in answer to any of your questions. Often what is *not* said is more revealing than what is.

The contract of employment

Any person you employ to work for more than 16 hours a week must have a contract of employment. The following points must be covered in the contract:

1. The job title.
2. The rate of pay and how it is calculated.

3. How frequently the money is to be paid.
4. The normal working hours and the terms and conditions relating to them.
5. Holidays and holiday pay.
6. Sick pay provision.
7. Pensions and pension schemes.
8. Term of notice required by both parties.
9. Any disciplinary rules relating to the job.
10. Grievance procedure.

Further information on the above can be obtained from a Social Security Office or Jobcentre, the title of the relevant leaflet being, 'Written statement of main terms and conditions of employment'.

Training staff

The value of training as an investment in staff cannot be overemphasised. Shop owners and managers sometimes see training as a waste of time because it does not necessarily produce quick results. The value of training is well illustrated by the gardener who went into a Woolworth store years ago and asked for a sack of seed potatoes. The assistant replied that, unfortunately, all the potatoes had shoots on them!

The best foundation for a good training programme is a proper introduction. Before the newcomer you selected at the interview accepts, you should have ready an overall (that fits), any necessary equipment, a copy of a simple training programme and the contract of employment. The first hour of the first day should, ideally, be concerned with the business itself, how it's organised and how the new recruit will fit in. Wages, deductions, staff discounts, hours, meal breaks, holiday entitlement and so on should be explained. The importance of punctuality and cleanliness should be stressed, particularly to younger recruits. The newcomer should be told that if there are any problems he or she should see you.

Both full- and part-time staff should be treated in this way because it gives them, early on, a sense of belonging. Building up loyalty of this kind is the very essence of training.

Any training could be done by you, but whoever is given the training job should see it as a responsibility, an honour even, and not a chore. Training means communicating to other people how they can best carry out their tasks. Too often 'training' and 'delegation' consist of a few hurried words to the newcomer to carry out such-and-such a task. Sometimes assistants go off without a clue of what to do because either they can't do it or they have misunderstood your request. First tell the trainees how to do the job; next show them how each step looks, giving practical advice at the same time; then let them try—and it's rarely too early for that; if necessary, coach the trainees when a mistake is made; lastly, when the points seem to have been learned competently, then step back—making sure that someone is around should difficulties arise. Make sure the trainees are progressing by check-testing from time to time and, of course, observing their work.

The points which have to be learned in basic training are:

Handling merchandise

1. How to unpack merchandise.
2. How to place new merchandise in the stock room.
3. Pricing and labelling.
4. Correct handling of merchandise.
5. Filling shelves and displays.
6. Age marking and rotation of stock.
7. Dusting and sweeping sales area.

Sales procedure

8. Cash register, giving change, taking cheques.
9. Filling in sales slips, other printed forms.
10. Wrapping and packing merchandise.
11. Weighing, measuring.
12. Range of goods and where to find them.

Making a sale

13. How to sell.
14. Communications, taking orders by telephone, etc.
15. Policy on delivery, posting, credit.
16. Handling complaints.

Technical terms

17. Explain trade terms and encourage newcomers to use them.

Dismissing staff

With the big increase in employee protection legislation many owners and managers, particularly of smaller firms, have been loath to take on new staff because of fears that they will be exposed to expensive legal action if they dismiss these employees. The present situation is not quite as bad as that. The

Employment Act 1980 excludes from a claim for alleged unfair dismissal any employee with less than two years' service in firms with less than 20 people. Even if your staff have not been with you for two years you must normally give one week's notice, or payment in lieu, unless the employee has been with you for less than four weeks. You can, however, dismiss summarily and without notice if the employee refuses to obey a reasonable instruction, seriously neglects his duties, is absent without permission or good cause, or if he is dishonest. It will be seen that there is considerable room for argument in these examples and if the employer is not sure that the necessary degree of misconduct has occurred he may prefer to give notice or wages in lieu. A number of pamphlets on this subject are available from Jobcentres.

Staff records

When you employ staff you become responsible for deducting PAYE tax from their wages and for seeing that the provisions of the Social Security Acts with regard to sick pay, unemployment benefit and so on are met.

The Inland Revenue have to be paid PAYE monthly and your office will send you a card to fill in. Remember to make a provision, keeping money back for tax (and for VAT), even if you have not been in touch with the tax office. Your local office of the Inland Revenue will supply you with tax tables and the employees' tax codes so that you can read off the appropriate deductions.

Each pay day each employee must be given an itemised statement showing gross wages, net wages, deductions and what they are for and details of part payments such as overtime rates.

At the end of the tax year (5 April) you will have to fill in two forms, summarising pay and deductions: the P60 which goes to the employee and the P35 which goes to the Inland Revenue. When an employee leaves you need to fill in a Form P45, and hand a copy to the employee concerned.

Two booklets worth reading, available at Jobcentres or from the Inland Revenue, before you start staff records are: *Guidance Notes on the Operation of PAYE* and *Employer's Guide to PAYE*.

National Insurance contributions are collected at the same time as PAYE and employers should obtain copies of the 'Employer's Guide to National Insurance Contributions' (leaflet NP 15) and 'National Insurance Contribution Rates' (leaflet

NI 208). These may be obtained from your local Department of Health or your local Social Security Office.

Checklist—what sort of person do I want?

1. What sort of help do I really need?
2. Do I want someone who can be left to work alone?
3. How much initiative do I want him or her to use?
4. Will there be much customer contact?
5. What sort of customers are they?
6. Does the job involve much contact with other staff?
7. What products are chiefly involved?
8. Is any previous knowledge of these products required? If so, how much?
9. Will there be any telephone work?
10. Will there be much cash handling?
11. Does the job entail much clerical work?
12. Is there any special equipment to use?
13. Are there any special aptitudes essential—or desirable?
14. What minimum educational qualifications are needed?
15. Is previous experience in a shop essential?
16. Will there be any cleaning to do?
17. Is there any driving?
18. Is there any heavy lifting?
19. What duties will most time be spent on?
20. What sort of person is the job likely to appeal to?
21. What pay, hours, holidays, training prospects can I offer that will make the right person want to work for me?
22. How important are age, sex, marital status, travelling arrangements etc?

Checklist of further employment legislation

Copies of these and other documents mentioned in the text can be obtained from HM Stationery Office.

Children and Young Persons Act 1983
Employment Acts 1980 and 1982
Employment Protection (Consolidation) Act 1978
Equal Pay Act 1970
Fair Wages Resolution 1946
Food Hygiene (General) Regulations 1970

Information for Employees Regulations 1965
Race Relations Act 1976
Rehabilitation of Offenders Act 1974
Social Security (Claims and Payment) Regulations 1979
Social Security Acts 1975, 1979, 1985 and 1986
Social Security Pensions Act 1975
Trade Union Act 1984
Unfair Contract Terms Act 1977
Wages Act 1986

Advisers, do you need them?

In a way, your advisers are part of your staff; after the problem of raising capital, another commonly mentioned drawback, particularly for sole traders, is not having anyone at hand in the business to give impartial advice on technical problems. Even staunchly independent people who say that they are going it alone need advisers. This is tied in with the fact that most of us have only a limited number of skills. Could we, for example, run our shop successfully *and* audit and produce a set of accounts which the taxman will accept? Maybe, but think of the extra time this would take which we could use for earning more profit in our shop. Most businesses, therefore, use at least four key people to advise them—an accountant, a bank manager, a solicitor and an insurance broker.

Choosing advisers

Make sure from the start that your advisers will take an impartial view of your problems. Clearly, this will mean excluding friends and relations whose judgement at times of crisis may become clouded emotionally. Of course, you may become good friends with your advisers over time, but this should happen after you have developed a good working relationship with them.

Bank manager

A major reason why 10 per cent of bank customers change their banks at least once in their lifetime is their branch manager. The big clearing banks are much of a muchness in their policies and in the services they provide, but their management development systems do mean that branches have management changes from time to time. Managers vary in terms of training and temperament: some have been better trained than others to understand the needs of small business. Such managers may seem initially off-putting when they ask you for things like management accounts and cash flow projections; in the long run you may well do better with them because they genuinely want to see your business growing on a sound footing and will look for ways to help you.

Visit your bank manager at least twice a year; some people see him once a month and even take him out to lunch. Send him copies of your accounts and develop your relationship as far as possible. If after all this courtship he still doesn't show much interest, offer your business around the other banks and tell your bank manager what you are doing. You need to be more than a number or an entry in a ledger because you never know when you may need your bank manager's goodwill.

Other professional advisers

Choosing an accountant, solicitor or insurance broker is different. You are not bound to go to a big organisation as you have to do in banking. There are several reasons why you should not. Big firms have large overheads and they need their big clients for their fees and commissions. Although many big practices have tried to adjust themselves to dealing with small clients they understand big business best and may not understand your occasional need for someone to hold your hand.

At the other end of the scale, avoid one-person firms because there are likely to be times when you want to see him, or her, and the person is on holiday, or ill, or out of town on another client's business. Two- or three-person partnerships are better because they will normally have someone to help and one partner who knows your business well.

Find likely advisers by asking around your own business friends and contacts or, if you are happy with him, your bank manager. A look in Yellow Pages or an enquiry at your local library may help. Points to look out for:

1. Membership of well-known professional associations with ethical standards.
2. Understanding of small businesses and, if possible, small retail shops.
3. Some entrepreneurial flair of their own; advisers who are not over-cautious and unimaginative.
4. A good track record in dealing with businesses like your own (insofar as you can find out information on this).
5. Advisers who will understand you and your motivations, while having enough professional impartiality to temper any over-optimism you may occasionally display.

6. Offices within easy reach of your own business.

Don't be overawed by advisers. You want to feel sufficiently at ease to challenge advice, ask for explanations and explore alternatives.

Remember, if you do think you have made a mistake in choosing any adviser, you can always change, but you should not do this too often. When you find people you are happy with, stick with them.

Chapter 6
Legal Requirements

Retail shops are subject to all sorts of regulations, some of them general and applicable to most businesses; a few are specific to the retail industry. Two important threads have developed in the law as it affects retailers. One concerns the sale of goods, regulations for which date back certainly to 1226 in Britain, while the other concerns the status of employees within the industry which has been subject to legislation only since 1912. Laws of both kinds have been increasing in volume and complexity during the past 10 years and this chapter discusses some of the most important acts, but not by any means comprehensively. A useful book to have by you is *Law for the Small Business* (7th edition) by Patricia Clayton and published by Kogan Page.

You are advised to consult a solicitor for definitive opinions and information on legislation affecting your shop. Government departments publish booklets and leaflets outlining and explaining much of the legislation which may affect you and many of them are mentioned in this chapter.

Consumer protection

Sale of goods. The Sale of Goods Act 1893 is crucial to the retailer simply because so much time is taken up by the sale and purchase of goods. First, the Act and the case law developed from it say that you must have 'good title' to goods before you can sell them; in other words, the goods must not be stolen, otherwise you won't have a legal right to sell them. Second, the goods you offer for sale must be as described, say, in a catalogue or advertisement when the buyer has not had the opportunity of seeing the goods first. ('Switch' selling, where an acceptable sample shown to the buyer is replaced by an inferior article of the same type, is now banned.) Third, the goods must be of 'merchantable' quality and reasonably fit for their proper purpose. Because many retailers were able to avoid the original Act's provisions by blaming defects on the manufacturers, the *Employment Protection Act 1975.* This is a complicated piece of

Supply of Goods (Implied Terms) Act was passed to plug these loopholes in the law. Under this Act goods sold 'in the course of business' must be of merchantable quality except for any specific defects brought to the buyer's attention before purchase. The retailer also cannot take away the rights of the customer under the Sale of Goods Act by using 'small print' exclusions under guarantees, eg for repairs.

Food and Drugs Acts 1955 and 1976. The purpose of these Acts is to protect the consumer from the sale of inferior food products and bring together previous legislation on food, drugs, markets and cold stores. The Acts make it an offence to describe food falsely or to mislead customers about its nature, substance or quality, including nutritional value. Ingredients must be listed on the pack in order of their weight and for pre-packaged foods, this is done by the manufacturer.

Consumer Protection Acts 1961 and 1971. These Acts empower the Secretary of State for Consumer Protection to make regulations in respect of certain types of goods, eg oil heaters and fireguards, flame-resistant nightwear for children, electrical appliance wiring, colour codes and children's toys. Local authorities are responsible for protecting shoppers. Trading Standards or Consumer Protection Departments see that laws concerning trading are met and investigate complaints.

Weights and Measures Acts 1963 and 1976. These Acts regulate the testing of weighing and measuring equipment and state how particular goods must be sold by weight or have the weights marked on labels. With unit pricing regulations today, both the price and the net weight of goods have to be on the pack so that customers have the opportunity of calculating the cost per gramme or ounce. Weights and Measures Inspectors or—as they are now called—Trading Standards Inspectors are employed by local authorities and can make tests or inspections, under the Acts, on a wide variety of consumer goods as well as weighing scales and the like.

Resale Prices Acts 1964 and 1976. The 1964 Act made it unlawful for individual producers as well as collective suppliers of goods to fix minimum prices. Today the only retail traders affected by resale price maintenance are booksellers and those shops which sell newspapers and magazines. Apart from these exceptions the retailer is not bound by anyone except himself in the setting of prices.

Trading Stamps Act 1964. Although the popularity of trading stamps as a sales promotion method has declined in recent years, the Act is still relevant. It states that the cash value of the individual stamp must be marked on its face and also makes it possible for customers to receive this cash value rather than gifts. The Act obliges shops offering stamps to display notices stating the cash value of the stamps and to keep, for public inspection, a copy of the promoter's current gift catalogue.

Trade Descriptions Acts 1968 and 1972. These Acts further strengthen the sale of goods legislation and make illegal the application of a false description (as defined by the Acts) to any goods, or the selling of goods which have been falsely described or the giving of misleading information about the goods. Additionally, certain imported goods must be labelled with their country of origin.

Consumer Credit Act 1974. If you, as a retailer, offer credit in any way to customers you may be subject to this Act which was passed to protect consumers, particularly to let them know the exact rate of interest they have to pay on their loan.

The Act requires anyone carrying on a credit or hire business (for instance, TV rental) to obtain a credit licence. False or misleading advertisements are automatically illegal under the Act and a 'cooling off' period is allowed to customers after they have signed the agreement to allow for second thoughts. There are also restrictions on the repossession of goods by the retailer.

Shops Acts 1950 and 1965. These Acts are aimed at protecting shop employees from long hours and exploitation. They cover general opening hours, early closing days and Sunday trading. You can pick your early day but are obliged to display both this and the general opening hours on a notice readable from the shop entrance.

Offices, Shops and Railway Premises Act 1963. As an employer you need to register your shop with the local authority on a form known as OSR.1. The Act lays down certain minimum standards in shops covering comfort, hygiene, safety and fire precautions. A wider ranging Act is the Health and Safety at Work Act 1974.

Health and Safety at Work Act 1974. This most recent Act covering safety at work is very comprehensive and you are advised to check with your local Health and Safety Executive Officer. The Act covers not only your employees but also the general public who may be affected by the work of others.

legislation in five parts which is perhaps best known for the rights it gives to unfairly dismissed employees. But there is a great deal more to it than that and you are referred to the list of pamphlets given in Chapter 5, page 47.

Insurance

The need for an insurance broker was mentioned in Chapter 5. There are many things to insure in your business and in some cases it may be illegal not to take out insurance against claims or losses. For example, you have a liability as an employer under the Employers' Liability (Compulsory Assurance) Act 1969 which requires employers to buy approved insurance policies with authorised insurers against liability for bodily injury or disease sustained by their full- and part-time employees in the course of their work. Your customers may also claim against you under public liability insurance if they have an accident in your shop. The shop premises, fixtures and fittings and stock also need insuring along with your plate glass shop window. You may also insure against loss of profits (in an extreme case your shop could be shut by a local health inspector) and against ill health which prevents you from running the business. Your insurance broker should be able to secure the best deals at lowest cost for you if you have a word with him.

Checklist of further consumer protection legislation

Copies of these Acts and those mentioned in the text can be obtained from HM Stationery Office:

Accidents and Dangerous Occurrences Regulations 1980
Customs and Excise Act 1952
Fair Trading Act 1973
Fire Precautions Act 1946
Fire Precautions (Loans) Act 1973
Food Hygiene (General) Regulations 1970
Food Hygiene Amendment Regulations 1991
Food Labelling Regulations 1980
Food Safety Act 1990
Occupiers Liability Act 1959
Public Health Act 1976
Resale Prices Acts 1964 and 1976
Restrictive Trade Practices Acts 1956, 1968 and 1976
Theft Act 1968
Unsolicited Goods and Services Acts 1971 and 1975

Chapter 7

Buying

Buying stock for resale is the first part of the process of retail merchandising and is arguably the most important. Your shop is not going to be successful without the right products in it, no matter how expertly you sell them or how efficiently you keep your costs down.

This chapter rests on the answers to two questions:

1. What sort of merchandise do your customers want to purchase from you?
2. How can these wants be satisfied in a way that helps to maximise your profit?

It is essential to find the right answers to these questions because you will probably spend more on stock for resale than on any other item. Bad buying not only accumulates the wrong kind of stock for your shop, but also involves buying too little or too much of a particular merchandise line. Stock is money tied up and if you can't release it into profitable sales, then your whole business becomes threatened. It is difficult to over-estimate the importance of buying in retail.

Satisfying the customer

A perennial question asked of retailers is, 'Who decides what appears in the shop—the customer or the retailer?' The answer is that the clever retailer finds out what the customers want and buys just that. Of course, it would be wonderful to be able to stock every item in your chosen retail trade which your customers are likely to ask for, but this is clearly impossible in terms of space and, more importantly, in the amount of cash you would have to tie up in stocks. You may lose a few customers, but this loss is more than outweighed by the money saved on these extra stocks. A major aim of buying, then, is to see that you have the product lines in your shop which will satisfy the majority of your customers most of the time. Even if you don't have quite what a few customers want, your own salesmanship and personal advice can swing many of these customers on to a reasonably close substitute.

There are two basic ways of finding out what customers require. The first is to analyse sales, line by line of particular products, and this is discussed more fully on page 57. Clearly, lines which sell well are meeting with customer approval; less successful products are not. Second, customers themselves are an excellent source of information about their wants. Keep a pad of paper in the shop headed 'Wants'. Every time a customer asks for something you can't supply, jot it down. If it keeps appearing in the 'wants' book it may be a line worth buying; if you already stock the line, its appearance in the book indicates a stock out which should be investigated.

Ranging policy

The assortment of merchandise required for particular trades and markets can be looked at in two ways:

Deep ranging. 'Depth' in assortment describes a comprehensive selection of brands, sizes, styles, colours and prices within a particular generic class or family of products. Specialist shops such as in clothing, food and household products concentrate on providing a wide choice in a narrow merchandise range. In-depth stocking leads to lower stockturns, compensated for by high profit margins.

Broad ranging. 'Breadth' in stock assortment means a wide selection of different generic classes of product carried by the same non-specialist or general shop such as the Large Mixed Retailer. For example, an audio shop may begin stocking a few 'white' goods such as fridges and washing machines. Stockturn could well be higher from a broad merchandise assortment, but profit margins could be slimmer.

It is possible to try to combine both depth and breadth in ranging, in order to maximise profitability.

Stocking for profit

The second question we asked at the beginning of this chapter concerns the economies of buying. We have already seen that we have to please the customer, but we also have to do this at a profit. There are several ways of measuring the efficiency of your buying, but the really crucial one is stockturn. Stockturn means the rate at which a particular product line is being sold and is measured by dividing the period sale of the item by the average stock value. Say, for example, the retail sales of an individual line during the year were £5000 and the average stock (calculated as we did in Chapter 4) was £1000. £5000÷£1000=5 times. This means that the item is replaced 5 times in one year. This figure by itself means little because it has to be compared with the stockturn on other lines and, indeed, with the stockturn of an entire shop. By making these calculations it is possible to grade product lines into fast sellers, basic demand lines and slow sellers.

Fast sellers. These are the lines which turn their stock over into cash the quickest, they sell more easily and they produce the profit. It is a well-known statistical fact that in most businesses 80 per cent of total sales are produced by only 20 per cent of the lines carried. These are the fast sellers.

Basic demand lines. These are products which are in constant demand, like salt in the grocery store or polish in the shoe shop. Customers expect to find them in your shop and if they don't are likely to take their business elsewhere. By and large, these are 'bread-and-butter' lines which sell with some regularity over the year and provide a steady, basic profit.

Slow sellers. It's just as true of product ranges that 80 per cent of the lines carried produce only 20 per cent of the profit (the opposite of the 'fast sellers' above). Most businesses have slow sellers which duplicate better lines unnecessarily, tie up space and capital and bring down the overall rate at which stocks can be turned into profit.

You can identify the kind of stockturn you are achieving by counting stocks regularly either on a unit (actual number of items) or on a value (retail price x number of items) basis. This is not the same as the annual stocktaking—discussed in the next chapter—and the method means only taking a small section of the shop at a time, until eventually the whole shop is covered. Only the best sellers need frequent counts, the rest, less often. A rough guide to the frequency of counting might be at least once a week for fast sellers, 4 to 6 weeks for moderate sellers and 6 to 12 weeks for the rest. Of course, special items such as fashion merchandise often need watching daily.

In order to obtain these facts efficiently, it is as well to tackle the job in easy stages, for example by taking one product group, such as biscuits or portable TVs at a time, and this will be aided by good organisation and layout in your shop and stockroom.

On the basis of these facts you will then be able to eliminate the really slow sellers and, because the monitoring system should be continuous, to keep them out. These lines will only sell a few items a year. They may give you a high gross profit margin but this is no real reason to keep them: you can sell lower margin substitute lines more quickly and make more overall profit. Make sure that you aren't duplicating lines: giving too much choice to the customer. Too much choice holds back potential fast sellers which might even include some basic demand lines. It is not unusual for such an exercise to reduce money invested in stock by 10 to 20 per cent.

How much to buy

You will need some kind of buying plan. One which is used by many independents is called the 'rate of stockturn' method. You will have projected your sales on a monthly basis, say, for the next year (as you did in your original business plan). Your average stockturn might be six times a year. This means that you have to keep two months' stock in hand at any one time. Every month, then, you will need to buy one month's stock at a level needed to support the next month's sales, as the table below shows:

	Jan £	*Feb* £	*Mar* £	*Apr* £	*May* £
Estimated sales	5,000	6,000	8,000	8,000	9,000
Purchases	6,000	8,000	8,000	9,000	

We are assuming here that you can get reasonably fast delivery of the goods you order; of course, if you use a cash-and-carry warehouse there is no problem except the capacity of your van or estate car. Your buying budget has to be reduced by the percentage gross margin because sales estimates are at selling value and purchases at cost, eg wholesale.

Trevor Beer breaks all the rules on planned buying in his dress shop. He makes little attempt to relate stockholding to turnover in the conventional ways described here. In this trade he can afford to because he can put unsold stock into his twice-yearly sales and still more than cover the purchase price. His labels are, however, of the haute couture variety such as Escada, Frank Usher, Puccini and Yves St Laurent. Notwithstanding this, Trevor says that many dresswear shops fail to perform well because the owner skimps on stock, not only initially but all the way through. There is a lesson here for many other retail shops, provided that they can successfully mark down bad buys. One or two retail trades are fortunate in that they can operate on a sale or return basis. Newsagents can send back their unsold newspapers and perhaps a third of their weekly magazines.

When to buy

When you have seasonal peaks and troughs in your sales you will need to watch timing. A frequent error made even by big multiples is to buy in stocks too early. This not only reduces stockturn but creates space problems and cuts down the buying budget for new lines which may appear later.

Obtaining supplies

Let us take two different situations. First, the shopkeeper might be taking over an existing business. Second, the shopkeeper might be starting up a new business in a retail trade (but if this is your situation do read the following section).

In the first instance, the retailer is likely to continue for a time with the existing suppliers, but this does not mean that these suppliers should not be analysed and appraised. It may be possible to improve the supply of goods for resale. You should get to know a good deal about your suppliers and not just those dealt with today but those who could be used in the future. It is worth remembering the big multiple groups who give the fewest possible suppliers the maximum trade each: as a result they can demand and receive better service, as described below. On the other hand it is usually more risky to obtain all supplies from a single source because the retailer is then too dependent on one firm.

The questions that need asking are, 'Have I got the right suppliers?' and, 'Have I got too many suppliers?' To answer these, list all the suppliers you use. The total may be surprisingly large. See what each supplier sends you, particularly the fast sellers, and what each *could* supply (by reference to their catalogues and price-lists). You may find that most supply a very limited selection. So you could have a choice of several suppliers who could each deliver a high proportion of your fast sellers. Some of these may be able to supply most of your other lines as well—if so, these may be the suppliers to favour. Next, compare prices. If you concentrated your buying, particularly of your fast sellers, into fewer suppliers, would you qualify for better terms? More credit? Extra discounts?

Delivery frequency is also important. Your suppliers' job, whether they are manufacturers or wholesalers, is to hold bulk stocks and deliver to retailers in convenient quantities and at frequent intervals. Take a tip from Marks & Spencer who insist that their suppliers keep stocks in their warehouses for ready delivery. This not only reduces money tied up in stock but also helps turn stock over faster. Which suppliers, then, can offer you more frequent deliveries? Just as important is the time taken between placing and receiving the order—is this lead time fast? By concentrating your buying with only two or three suppliers instead of six or ten, you could well 'bargain' for more frequent deliveries. Their costs don't necessarily have to go up as much as the profit from the regular, guaranteed business you are offering them. This, in turn, should improve the supplier's loyalty to you. Some suppliers are not very dependable. In spite of all the promises over the telephone, they may let you down too frequently. Look also at the amount of promotion the supplier (usually the manufacturer) is putting behind the product. Fast moving lines or brand new lines usually have the best support.

Now let us turn to people who are setting themselves up in retail business for the first time. Much of what we have already discussed about buying is applicable once the shopkeeper has started business. We can summarise, however, by saying: first, concentrate your buying into as few suppliers as possible, and second, use the buying power you obtain to secure extra discounts, more frequent deliveries and better, more loyal service.

When starting a business from scratch it is necessary to find suitable suppliers. Merchandise for sale is obtainable from wholesalers, certain manufacturers selling direct to retailers, importers and agents (such as food brokers) and in certain merchandise fields such as antiques, jewellery and plate, the public remains an important source of supply. Sometimes it is possible to buy from a cash-and-carry warehouse or to obtain supplies by joining a voluntary group (see pages 63-4 for a discussion of these two sources).

When choosing suppliers the following points should be borne in mind:

1. Do they have a good range of products, including brand names, at a reasonable price?

2. Will they deliver fairly often and make special deliveries in an emergency?
3. Do they offer advice and information to retailers, for example on how to make your shop more profitable, as well as promotional aids and nationwide advertising?

Salespeople—help or hindrance?

If you are running a small shop today it is inevitable that you will be approached by sales representatives from time to time. Their prime aim, of course, is to convince you to place an order with them. If they have properly assessed your needs then it may be advantageous to you to buy from them, but if they are merely after commission they can not only waste your time but provide you with an even bigger problem. In one case quoted recently a personable young salesman entered a shop in Herefordshire and told the owner that no village shop should be without a stock of bootlaces. The owner bought £100 worth and received a radio alarm clock as a reward. Said the shopkeeper, 'At the end of the year the clock no longer worked and I had sold just £10 worth of bootlaces, leaving another nine years to get the rest of my money back.'

Approaches from salespeople should be dealt with on their merits. This is not to say that reps should be treated discourteously. It is often useful to make a friend of a salesperson once the initial orders have proved to be profitable. Desperately needed stock orders can sometimes be given priority if a good relationship exists between buyer and seller. Salespeople may also offer useful point of sale material and help to organise special shop and window displays for their company's products, proffering helpful advice on the way.

But in the end, only the retailer can judge the real value of the salesperson's efforts and this will come out in sales and profitability. Make sure your suppliers' salespeople understand how you are trying to run your business. Then they will be less inclined to attempt to persuade you to buy more than you need. Many salespeople do not understand the ways in which retailers can make most profit because they are concerned largely with their own products in the shop. On the other hand, the good salesperson does understand retailing and can help. Use intelligently the sales representatives who visit you. They can tell you of activity which can help you to adjust orders, take advantage of special promotions and so on.

New product lines

Today, especially, a constant stream of new products enters the market. The retailer must try to keep track of them for three very good reasons. First, some new products are extremely successful and may add considerably to overall profitability. Second, it is important to replace the 'dead' lines or slow sellers as far as possible with fresh new lines. In other words, the continuous introduction of new, successful lines will help to increase the proportion of best sellers. Third, customers usually expect a shop to keep up to date. After all, unless your business is dynamic it will die.

New lines, then, are vital to a business. This is not only true of fashion goods which change in style regularly, but of most other types of business, too. New lines can be those which have been on the market for some time but which you have not sold before, or genuinely new lines such as the fabulously successful 'Yorkie' chocolate bar or the microwave oven. It has been estimated that in many businesses up to 20 or 30 per cent of their turnover in a year comes from lines which were not stocked in the previous year.

Talking with manufacturers' and wholesalers' representatives is one way in which you can keep yourself in the picture about new lines—and you probably won't need to ask them! Look at the trade press and mail shots from your suppliers. Use a 'wants' slip system. Last, but not least, look at other stores which can afford to carry bigger selections. Most big retailers carry out these 'competition checks' on other shops. You can be sure that if certain lines are placed in good positions and displayed prominently, these are successful sellers.

At the end of the day, however, it will be your judgement as a retailer that will determine whether to stock these lines or not. You will have to know something about local tastes which may make a line more or less suitable for you. Big retailers have the resources to adopt a 'suck it and see' attitude. Marks & Spencer, again, put new products in about 20 (out of their total of 260) stores to see how they sell. Clearly the small independent retailer with a single shop cannot do this, so it is well to go carefully and order a basic minimum to start with. The following checklist may help you to judge the worth of a new line:

1. Does it conveniently fit any one of my merchandise groups?
2. Does it really add to my stock assortment rather than merely duplicate existing lines?

3. Is it equal or better value than existing lines?
4. Will it suit enough of my customers; has it any special extra appeal?
5. Is there any proof that it will sell? Has it been test marketed? Are other stores selling it successfully?
6. Does it come from a reputable manufacturer?
7. Is it well packaged and attractive?
8. Is it well known, well promoted?
9. Does the margin compare favourably with other lines? Or better?
10. Is there an opening bonus to allow me to 'chance my arm' and mark it down if it doesn't sell?

Keep a careful check on the new line, recording unit sales on a daily basis for two or three weeks, remembering that seasonal patterns may affect them. On this basis you can decide whether to reorder (and how much) or to 'kill' the line.

Voluntary group trading

Although the buying aspect is only one advantage of voluntary group membership, it is an important one. Most voluntary groups in Britain have been started by wholesalers. Wholesalers have seen their traditional markets declining due to the growth of the multiple retailer which now often buys direct from the manufacturer and operates its own warehouses. The increase in multiple power has also led to a decline in the numbers of small retailers which really do need the support of wholesalers. A voluntary group recruits a corps of retailers, usually in a particular trade and buys on behalf of these retail members. The advantages to a number of these 'symbol' groups are:

(a) Bulk buying by the group means bigger discounts which are passed on to retail members in the form of lower prices to compete with the multiples.
(b) The problems of buying administration are largely taken from the group member.
(c) In larger group wholesale chains, national advertising, sales promotion and point-of-sale material boosts turnover, supported by group 'own brand' merchandise.
(d) Financial assistance and advice on retailing methods are available to the member.

For a small, relatively limited range shop, there are clear

benefits in membership, but this is balanced by the need to place a minimum weekly order with the group warehouse. Voluntary groups are found extensively in the grocery trades, but they have become popular with many other independent retailers, notably chemists, hardware stores, clothing and footwear shops, CTNs (confectioner-tobacconist-newsagent) and toy shops.

Cash-and-carry warehouses

The cash-and-carry warehouse is normally also run by a wholesaler and its customers are retailers who are given a special card which allows them to buy at wholesale prices. Payment is always in cash (or by cheque) and customers are expected to take their own goods away with them. These warehouses are normally organised on a self-service basis and are rather like a big supermarket.

The cash and carry offers a number of advantages to the retailer:

1. Buying prices are quite keen.
2. A shopkeeper can buy as necessary and use the warehouse as his stockroom—thus helping his stock turnover.
3. Time can be saved in dealing with representatives, checking goods, invoices and so on.
4. The warehouse layout gives a much better knowledge of what products are available.
5. Contact with the wholesaler is improved.

The disadvantages are:

1. The time saved by not having to deal with representatives and check goods and invoices may be lost in going back and forth to the cash and carry.
2. Transport is at the retailer's expense.
3. You may have to pay staff extra to cover your absence.
4. You may have to do your own loading and unloading.
5. Goods have to be paid for at the time—there are no credit facilities.

Large cash-and-carry groups like Makro and Trademarkets now carry many non-food lines and this may interest retailers other than independent grocers. Look at your local Yellow Pages for wholesalers in each trade along with cash-and-carry warehouses.

Further tips on finding suppliers if consulting directories doesn't bear fruit are:

1. Ask your trade association, if you are a member, or the relevant wholesalers' association for a list of wholesalers in your area.
2. If you wish to stock goods manufactured in a particular country, enquire at that country's Chamber of Commerce. You may find that the foreign firm is already represented here and that stocking the goods would be relatively easy.
3. Advertisements in the trade press or the Yellow Pages suggest possible suppliers.

Chapter 8
Stock Management

Stock is any product item which is owned by the retailer but which has not yet been sold. Stock is found on the shelves of the shop and in the stock-room. You probably put more money into your stock than into any other part of your business because it is the only part which produces profit for you. The secret of good retailing is to turn stock into profit as quickly as possible. Stock management is of great importance to the retailer because:

1. It tells you what is selling and what is not selling so that you can buy the right range of goods for your shop.
2. It helps you to reduce the total amount of cash tied up in stock.

Product line stockturns

Chapter 7 mentioned the need for the retailer to check what happens to individual lines in terms of stockturn. This information helps you to buy a profitable range of products for your shop.

An example of stockturns for various trades is given on page 67.

Stock-sales relationship

This relationship shows what is happening to your business in terms of stock turnover. We have already noted that the carrying of too much stock not only ties up too much 'dead' capital but reduces the ability of the business to convert this cash into profitable sales. The easiest way of checking out this relationship is to use the existing system of control and add to it. You probably keep a book in which you record your weekly sales figures, or cash banked. Rule a column beside these figures and put in the total of your week's purchases. Use these facts as an early warning system. Totalled over a month they will show clearly how your sales are moving in relation to your buying. If your sales start slowing down but your buying comes on at the same rate there could be money wasted in excessive stocks. Like many things in retailing, stock checks take a little more time, but the extra effort enables you to get a grip on the business and thus the effort pays for itself many times over.

Average stockturns for various retail trades

Trade	*Average number of times stock is turned per annum*
Food shops	
Small grocers	14
Dairies	95
Butchers	63
Fishmongers, poulterers	90
Greengrocers, fruiterers	51
Bread and flour confectioners	40
Off-licences	10
Clothing and footwear shops	
Footwear	4
Men's and boys' wear	5
Women's, girls' and children's wear	5
General clothing	5
Leather and travel goods	4
Household goods retailers	
Household textiles	5
Carpets	7
Furniture	5
Electrical, gas and music goods	6
Hardware, china and fancy goods	4
DIY	6
Other retailers	
Chemists	7
Booksellers, stationers	6
Photographic goods	5
Jewellers	2
Toys, hobby, cycle, sports goods	4
Florists	7
Confectioner/tobacconist/newsagents	12

Source: Retail Inquiry 1984

Stock control

The importance of controlling merchandise has already been made clear. It involves the maintenance of a correct balance between the assortment of merchandise carried and the sales to which it gives rise. The aim is to obtain as big a turnover as possible with the most economic inventory (stock) level. There is a clear indication that the rate of stockturn has a decisive effect on the profitability of a retail business. As an example, let us take two retailers, both of whom have £10,000-worth of stock at selling value and whose average gross profit margin is 20 per cent. If retailer A sells and replaces his stock six times a year his sales are £10,000 x 6=£60,000 and his gross profit is £12,000 (£60,000 x 20 per cent). Retailer B sells and replaces his stock eight times a year so his sales are £80,000 and his profit is £16,000 (£80,000 x 20 per cent). Assuming the running costs of both shops to be £8,000, retailer A makes a net profit of £4000 while retailer B makes double this at £8000.

Stocktaking

'Taking stock' involves the counting and valuing of every item of stock at a given time. It is different from a 'stock check', which is designed to identify quickly rates of sales in fast-moving merchandise. Stock-taking is also different from 'stock calculation' where the last value of stock is added to purchases and the subsequent figure deducted from sales to give an approximate value of current stock. The main objective of all three ways of observing and recording stock is to maintain a correct balance between stock levels and sales. We have already seen that too much cash tied up in stock can severely reduce the profitability of a business.

Stock needs to be taken once a year in order to produce a value for the stock asset in the final accounts and balance sheet. It also defines true stockturn rates, isolates fast- and slow-selling lines, establishes the true gross margin of the business and identifies true stock losses.

Stocktaking can be undertaken by valuers on your behalf, but even if you carry it out by yourself to save money it can interfere with customer service. The best time to do it is after the shop has closed or on Sundays.

Ordering

You must set the level of stock for each line which is the lowest you can keep continuously and with reasonable safety to meet normal demand. This will depend on how fast the line sells and how fast it can be replaced. Let's take an example of a product which sells between 50 and 70 a week. Let's assume an average sale of 60 per week. Let's further assume that it normally takes four weeks from the time you place the order to the time you receive delivery. It is probably wise to add on another week to the four weeks' delivery time in case of holidays, sickness or other causes of delay. The re-order level will be five weeks x 60 to cover the period during which you will be waiting for delivery. So you should re-order 300 units (5 x 60) and if the line has to be ordered in, say, 24-unit orders or cartons, you will need to order 13 cartons, rounding up to the nearest order quantity. If the rate of sale remains the same the line will need to be re-ordered immediately the delivery arrives. If the delivery has arrived on time only four weeks' sales need to be ordered (one week's safety stock will still be in hand) to keep to the five weeks' minimum safe stock level. If, however, the rate of sale increases, your regular stock check on fast sellers will show this up immediately and you would order as soon as the minimum safe stock level was reached. Don't order above these levels unless sales start increasing dramatically.

There are some risks in keeping stock levels low. You should watch for any likelihood of a seasonal rise in sales. Christmas is clearly a time during which sales in all trades rise, but there are other seasonal peaks like Easter (for Easter eggs) and early November (for fireworks). Certain times of the year in certain trades are all-important as far as sales are concerned. It also pays to keep a special watch out for manufacturers' advertising or promotional campaigns which usually last for only one or two weeks but which can produce profitable results. Sometimes there are supply problems. Demand for a certain line can outstrip production, deliveries can break down, wholesalers can misjudge demand and so on. You should not hold excess stocks just in case any of these things happen, but you can keep close tabs on what is happening and so can be forewarned of trouble.

The holding of stock, along with buying, selling and shop layout, is fundamental retailing and it links closely with the other three functions.

Incoming goods

The point at which goods enter the shop must be subject to controls and for very clear reasons. A retailer is well advised, first, to make a specific and trustworthy member of staff responsible for all incoming merchandise. Before delegating these tasks, you should show the subordinate exactly what is to be done. One of the best forms of training is training by example.

First of all, try to ensure that all deliveries are made to one point. Keep this area clear so that deliveries can be checked and handled speedily and efficiently. Thoroughly examine all the goods. If there is anything wrong with them, notify the supplier immediately and mark the delivery note accordingly.

Thoroughly check the consignment by counting that your goods correspond exactly with the information on the delivery note. Keep the delivery note for comparison with the invoice to make sure that you are only paying for what you have received. Compare the delivery with your order. Has an item which sells well been substituted for a slower seller? If you are in any way dissatisfied with the quantity, contact the supplier and, if needs be, return merchandise which is not of the standard ordered.

If a particular manufacturer or wholesaler is frequently out of stock or delivers the wrong amounts or the wrong qualities or is late in his deliveries, there is often a case for changing your supplier.

The effort and time spent on controlling goods inward is well worth while. Errors can be time-consuming, leading to missed sales and dissatisfied customers. But this is not the only thing that may cost you money. The theft of two bottles of shampoo from your shelves may cost you £2. One order of shampoo invoiced but not delivered could cost you £24. Most studies carried out show that 60 per cent of stock loss is from the back of the shop.

Price marking

It is convenient, very often, to price the goods received as they enter the shop or in the stockroom. The object of 'marking off' is to record merchandise information on the article itself or the container, for use in stock control or to inform the customer.

The type of merchandise, the information to be recorded and the method of presentation will all determine the method and media of marking off and standard methods include:

1. Swing tickets such as Kimball tags
2. Pin and clip-on tickets
3. Gum tabs (often automatically stuck on with a price-marking gun)
4. Pressure and heat-adhesive labels
5. Direct marking methods, eg rubber stamps or fibre-tip markers.

Shopfitters listed in Yellow Pages should be able to give advice and provide catalogues. The trade journals often contain advertisements for price tickets and other sundries.

The stock-room

The need for stock-room space varies from one retail trade to another and between various methods of retailing. Very often goods cannot all be sold as soon as they are received, or be kept on display from the time they are delivered until the time they are sold.

It is worth asking yourself whether you need much stock-room space or, indeed, any at all. Sales and profits are not made in stock-rooms. It is best, if possible, to feature as much merchandise as possible in the shop and keep reserve stock to a minimum. Better stock control will help you to make better use of precious space, which could be incorporated in the selling area.

Another way of checking whether stock-room space is being properly used is to investigate the lines on your stock-room shelves; some of them may not be worth carrying. There are four categories of merchandise which you might find in this inspection. First, slow-selling lines: products with a very slow rate of sale do not earn their keep and tie up money that could be used profitably elsewhere. Second, duplicated lines: these lines sell slowly because customers prefer similar products with a better known brand name. Third, 'forgotten lines': some kinds of merchandise end up in the stock-room after an unsuccessful promotion or after the Christmas rush and then become 'buried' in a corner. These lines are often not worth keeping and may even have deteriorated. Lastly, 'limited life' lines: high stocks of seasonal lines at the end of their season are out of place in the stock-room. Clear out all these lines by offering them as 'sale' or 'special' lines or, if they cannot be sold, throw them away.

This sort of clearance will not only provide you with a more profitable stock assortment but will give you space for more profitable use.

Using stock-rooms efficiently

Use of space. Wall areas should be used to the maximum, with free-standing racks allowing sufficient aisle width for trolleys and bulky items; fullest use of floor-to-ceiling height should be attempted.

Flexibility. Added flexibility of wall space can be gained by using one of the various types of adjustable shelving systems for stock-rooms; these allow you to adjust shelf space and allocate sections to specific products.

Accessibility. All stock should be as accessible as possible and the faster-selling and heavier items should be as near the sales area as possible.

Grouping. Lines should be stacked so that they follow the same pattern and layout as the shop; this will naturally involve grouping allied products together (the only exceptions may be the really bulky or fast-selling lines); this method of layout is often seen in grocery and pharmacy stock-rooms and also in shops with a self-service layout.

Space allocation. Maintain only the minimum safe stock level of each line and allocate just enough space for it; gaps will become immediately obvious.

Identification. As far as possible lines should be kept in outer packs or cases, each properly marked with the contents; each section allocated should also be marked with the product name and other details, if necessary, and this will help in stock counts.

Rotation. Old stock should be moved into the sales area before new stock to reduce the risk of deterioration.

Reception. An adequate space for handling, checking and unpacking the goods as they are delivered is required so that the new goods are kept apart from old stock until the reception procedure is completed.

Tidiness. A stock-room should be kept as clean and tidy as possible at all times; gangways should be kept clear, particularly if the fire exit is off the stock-room.

Security. All lines should be placed in visible positions if possible and lighting should be adequate; for high value items like tobacco and small electrical appliances some form of cage or lockfast store may be necessary.

Staff. Consider the welfare of your staff, particularly where female labour is concerned; you cannot expect them to lift very heavy weights or to work in cramped areas. Staff should also be trained in the rules suggested above.

Chapter 9
Selling

Selling is the process where, through a stage of information-giving and persuasion, a customer agrees to a transaction by which the ownership of goods moves from the shop to the customer, in return for payment. Selling is the end product of all the operations which go towards the merchandising process and is thus of vital importance in the retail shop. Selling can be either personal or impersonal.

Personal selling

Personal service is found largely in counter-service shops such as jewellers, many kinds of small food shops such as bakers, and any place where the product sold does not lend itself easily to open, self-service displays. Personal service is when a customer tells the salesperson what his needs are. In this face-to-face situation the salesperson explores the customer's needs, explains, informs, persuades and demonstrates merchandise in order to bring about a transaction which is satisfactory to the customer and profitable to the shop.

Customer motivation

Customers buy products for many different reasons and it may help you to know what the specific motivation is in any particular situation. Motivation is based on the satisfaction of physical needs (eg a cold drink on a hot day), recreation and comfort (sales of leisure goods, for instance, are booming today), imitation (cosmetics and clothing as used by, say, Selina Scott), exclusiveness (high-priced items whose ownership bolsters the ego of the possessor), family affection (toys for children), health (organically grown foods), habit (tobacco), novelty and so on. A retailer who recognises the motivations listed above can appeal in a general manner through advertising, sales promotion and shop image to potential customers.

Product appeal

The motivations for buying may also be modified by other factors which will influence choice. The sources of goods sometimes have strong buying recommendations (eg Harris Tweed, German kitchen equipment). Price is almost invariably an important factor, particularly with lower income groups; customers balance price against their subjective idea of value. Articles are also sold for what they do as well as for what they are, so performance is important, as is durability where some customers will be prepared to pay more for goods which have a longer useful life. What may be cheap to buy may be expensive to use, but a total saving can be made over a long period if you can assist a customer in choosing a quality which is economical to run, even if the cost is high at the outset. Ease of maintenance and the availability of after-sales service also figure in customers' minds when buying.

Customer attitude

Although the general motivation of customers and the appeal of products are useful in helping you to sell, the personal selling process must start off with the 'weighing up' of the individual customer. Customer attitudes must be identified so that the right approach is made. Basic customer types are as follows:

1. *The 'just looking' customer.* This type of customer may well be browsing or comparing prices and qualities. Too many sales assistants, even today, are told to ask, 'Can I help you?' With customers of this kind such an approach can send them right out again.
2. *The decisive customer.* Such customers present few difficulties to sales staff because they have already made up their minds what they want. They should be served as quickly as possible. The attitude of this customer type tends to reinforce positiveness in the sales assistant who may then start overselling which not only wastes time but could lose the sale.
3. *The uncertain customer.* This type of customer needs reassurance, backed by extensive product knowledge as required.
4. *The talkative customer.* Time spent in conversation, particularly at peak selling periods, could mean lost sales elsewhere. Tact and firmness are required to bring

the customer back to the merchandise and its selling points.

5. *The silent customer.* Without clues to the customer's opinions about merchandise, plenty of sales talk is necessary, with the customer free to handle merchandise so that his or her intentions can be gauged.
6. *The disagreeable customer.* This type of customer should be shown the full range of stock available and be given a brief sales talk, but the customer should otherwise be given most of the chance to do the talking. Unreasonable remarks should not be taken personally by the retailer and any apologies due for previous poor service should be given.
7. *The opinionated customer.* The opinions offered, even if factually incorrect, should rarely be challenged and patience is a watchword here.
8. *The suspicious customer.* Suspicion is sometimes produced by a disappointing purchase made previously in the shop. You should try to allay the suspicion and build up the customer's confidence again. Firms like Marks & Spencer offer to exchange a faulty article or even an undesired article or, if requested, may make a full refund.

We now cover the points that take in the opening, continuing and closing of the sale in personal selling. (In the non-personal sale there is little or no customer contact.)

The approach

As we have seen, by correctly spotting the particular customer's demeanour, you can adopt the appropriate style of contact. Remember the customer is the most important person in your shop. Without customers a shop cannot survive. When a customer approaches a salesperson, this should not be regarded as a work interruption—rather the customer is the purpose of the work. Customers should be treated in the way that we all like to be treated. Their dislikes are often our dislikes. Customers like a cheerful smile, politeness, pleasant personality and to be treated as someone special. They do not, obviously, warm to rudeness, curtness, indifference or being ignored. (Although the retailer will know these things, it is important to inculcate staff with these ideas during their early training.)

The customer's first impression of the person who will sell to them is important. A dirty and unkempt appearance gives the idea that the salesperson does not care about the job. No credence will be given. An insincere attitude undermines belief and confidence immediately and so the salesperson must try to communicate an attitude of sincerity. A smile and a pleasant tone of voice communicate a friendly and helpful attitude. Overall, the salesperson's attitude should be determined by the customer, but the sales attitude shown should reflect service not servility. Another clue to the customer's attitude is 'body language' or their facial expressions and limb movements. This says a good deal about a person's mood. Similarly, salespersons must make sure that their own moods do not communicate the wrong impression through body language. Examples of body language include finger tapping and foot shuffling (annoyance, impatience), leaning on counters and fittings (lack of enthusiasm or alertness).

To continue with the actual selling process, the salesperson must know the customer's requirements before he or she can know the correct merchandise to present. Much of the information relating to the customer, such as economic standing, family size, specific reasons for purchase and so on should come out through observing and conversing with the customer. If the appropriate item is not in stock you may be able to offer a satisfactory substitute but this should not be pressed on the customer. In such a situation, or where the customer is amenable to purchasing higher-priced items in a range, 'selling up' is a possibility.

One of the key sections of the salesperson's presentation is the detailing of the benefits of the article, if the customer is concerned not so much with the product as with what satisfactions it will bring. In the same way that advertisements suggest that a product such as shampoo or toothpaste increases sex appeal, so the salesperson may stress the benefits of the product rather than the product itself. Someone selling a cooker, for example, may wax lyrical about the wonderful meals it can produce, almost as if the cooker can do so itself without help.

If the customer voices objections to the product, these should be dealt with competently and truthfully. Sometimes a customer may point out that the product can be bought more cheaply elsewhere. In such cases it is better not to suggest that the customer is free to go elsewhere but to thank him or her and state that this matter will be looked into. This is also a good time to stress any guarantees or after-sales benefits.

Facts should be given slowly and clearly; they are new to the customer. The selling points of the article which appeal most to the customer should be emphasised. By encouraging questions from the customer a multiple sale can be developed: this means that instead of buying just one item, the customer buys two, or more, often complementary products (eg a squash racket and a box of squash balls). The customer should be given the opportunity to handle the merchandise and 'try it out'. The merchandise itself should be handled by the salesperson with care; this emphasises how valuable it is. On the negative side, salespeople should never demonstrate merchandise on top of other products, nor should too many articles be presented at once. Those articles which have been rejected should be put aside or returned to their fittings (remember, in a counter-service shop stock should be as close to the assistant's hand as possible). Technical language should not be used in demonstrating products and a salesperson should also never deliberately mislead a customer; honesty builds goodwill. Merchandise should never be criticised even if it is low priced; the assistant may have to serve it a few minutes later. Customers prefer to believe that they are shopping at a first-class shop that stocks high quality goods.

Closing the sale

As with the initial approach, timing is essential and the sale must be concluded before interest wanes. The most important thing to remember about closing a sale is to act as if the sale is a foregone conclusion. Salespeople should not let the customer think that they are worried about whether or not a sale will be achieved. Sometimes it is difficult after all the points have been dealt with to bring the sale to a close. In these circumstances, and if it is appropriate, the salesperson may ask the customer to choose between two articles. On rare occasions a price reduction may be offered; more often the salesperson may state that the product is in demand, there are not many left and it is doubtful whether the manufacturers have any more.

If a sale is agreed, the salesperson must then be prepared to answer any questions as to methods of payment, delivery and aftersales service. If the sale is not agreed the salesperson should let the customer go gracefully. Customers should not be harangued or over-persuaded or they may never set foot in the shop again.

When the goods are being wrapped is the time to make a related sale. One successful sale is the foundation upon which to build another, but the retailer should discourage sales assistants from adding, 'Anything else, madam?' Rather, the salesperson should ask (for example when selling a video recorder) 'Do you require any blank tapes, madam?'

Related sales are usually of articles that complement the product sold; they are generally cheaper, so customers feel they are only spending a little more for something that is necessary. Secondary sales are just that and they should never be pushed, particularly if it is obvious that the customer is not interested and/or is in a hurry.

Impersonal selling

Over the past 20 years there has been a movement away from personal service towards self-selection and self-service. Impersonal service systems have become popular with retailers because they speed up customer flow, help increase sales, and reduce wage costs as a percentage of sales. Self-service is quite different from counter service in that the merchandise is openly displayed and there is no pressure by sales staff on customers to buy. The customer picks up the required merchandise himself and takes it to a check-out point where payment is made. Self-selection differs slightly from self-service in that each department or group of departments is provided with its own cash register, located either adjacent to the display fittings or at a cash-and-wrap station. Assistants are available in the department to answer customer queries and they also deter shoplifters. (Marks & Spencer operate all three kinds of selling system: food sections are on a self-service basis, textile sections on a self-selection basis and customer services for merchandise exchange on a counter-service basis.)

There are many advantages to a self-service or self-selection layout. Space is more economically used when space for serving is replaced by display area. The open displays of, usually, prepacked products sell themselves and provide more impulse purchases. More stock on the shop shelves means less stock held up in the stock-room where it cannot be seen and sold. Self-service trading is designed for a shop to be run with less experienced staff; few staff need be employed and sales per assistant are usually much greater than in a counter-service shop. Pilferage can actually be reduced in a properly designed and well run self-service shop, because of the improved sight lines and the greater proportion of stock on open display and under the gaze of the manager or proprietor. A common misconception of the self-service store is that it is not possible to provide personal service. In fact, staff may have more time to attend to queries from customers who need guidance. Conversion to self-service creates the excitement of a 'new' shop opening: presenting a modern, efficient image to customers while, at the same time, adding value to the shop. In summary we can say that the self-service shop looks better, is easier to run and, significantly, is a more profitable shop.

Checklist of steps to a sale

1. Have a thorough knowledge of the stock.
2. Always welcome the customer.
3. Be ready to give service, and if service is required find out customer needs by careful questioning.
4. Select a suitable product, based on your assessment of the customer.
5. Present it in terms of benefits, not just product attributes.
6. Allow customers to handle the product or self-demonstrate it.
7. Customer hesitation may suggest an objection. Discover any objections by further careful questioning and answer them honestly, again stressing benefits.
8. Close the sale when all objections have been dealt with.

Chapter 10

Shop Design, Layout and Display

A shop is merely a box with an entrance on to a street through which customers come and go and, usually, a rear entrance through which stock for resale is brought. The box is often rectangular, but it may be L-shaped. The idea of shop design is to attract customers into the shop from the street and to enhance the products on display, thereby encouraging customers to buy. Shop layout and display are extensions of design which make the most profitable use of space by allowing customers to find products easily or to find someone to sell them. Some shops have a particular quality which defies description, yet they convey to the public what kind of business they are in and, more important, an excitement for the products being sold. Let us look first at the 'box' in terms of shop design.

Frontage

The frontage or exterior of a shop is the customer's first view of it. If the exterior does not encourage a customer to enter, the best interior layout is wasted. Check that the fascia and paintwork are in a good state of repair and decoration. If the basic shop front is in good structural condition, revitalise it. Shop exteriors are expensive and inconvenient to change. Only if the whole frontage is unsuitable for your business (too much or too little glass, badly placed access and so on) should you rip it all out. There are, however, variations on a theme of frontage refurbishment. For example, it is surprising how much difference a modern illuminated sign can make. Either this could go the whole length of the frontage or an 'off the peg' standard sign could be purchased. An even cheaper option is to purchase a set of plastic lettering. Planning permission is needed for an illuminated sign, but your sign contractor would normally put this through for you. New doors can also make an enormous improvement. All customers will notice them on entering and leaving. British Home Stores (BhS) put new doors on their refurbished stores as part of a major redesign programme. Another important advantage in having a new entrance is that in so many cases it can replace a restricting lobby or arcade which, together with the removal of old window beds, could add another £100 per square foot on turnover. But if no amount of spring cleaning and minor alterations can improve the tired appearance of your shop front, a complete face-lift may be the answer. Remember that any expense can be put against tax, so the expenditure is not always as high in real terms as it seems at first.

To conclude on frontage, don't forget that, initially, you are selling from the street.

Colour

This is one main way of creating your shop's image. The way colour is used in a retail shop will depend on the trade, customer type and merchandise. For instance, outlets such as boutiques, record and gift shops selling fashion goods to the predominantly young benefit from exciting background colours. The colours you choose should help to complement the stock you are selling. It is perfectly feasible to use more than one colour, perhaps to provide dramatic contrasts, but do not use too many. Remember that the walls, flooring and ceiling must produce a coherent effect of blending or contrast. Colour can be used to change the apparent size of your shop. Light colours help a shop to appear open and roomy. Dark colours bring the walls 'close' together and provide a more intimate atmosphere. Research has shown that, although more difficult to keep clean, pastel shades provide the best working conditions. This is important, therefore, not only for customers but for staff as well.

Flooring

Flooring is expensive and is often a one-off purchase. Because you will not want to change it, flooring should be functional, hardwearing, easy to clean and inexpensive to maintain, especially if the shop is in a 'busy' trade with lots of customer circulation. Tiled floors made of material like PVC allow heavily worn areas to be replaced easily. Make sure that the flooring material is non-slip, wet or dry. Some trades such as fashion or footwear will need carpet because it looks and feels good, is sound absorbent and has the most customer appeal. Use the best quality carpet you can afford, and if there are heavy wear areas consider carpet tiles which have the obvious advantage of being movable. With carpet, watch for frayed edges which can easily cause accidents as well as being unsightly. Very light or very dark colours make for extra cleaning problems. Whatever flooring material you choose it should either blend or contrast with the overall decor of walls and ceiling.

Lighting

Good lighting is just as much part of your shop decor as the colour and materials of walls, floor and so on. It enables products to be seen properly and to the best advantage, and itself creates atmosphere. The cheapest and most efficient store illumination is still a variation of fluorescent lighting. There are many different warmths, colours and fittings available. All filament and fluorescent lights have a life expressed in hours of use and become inefficient or useless unless they are regularly changed. Tungsten spotlights can be used tactically for highlighting special areas or lightening 'dead' areas of the shop. When used in concentration, however, spots give out a disturbing amount of heat and this should be watched in shops with poor ventilation. If you are rewiring have plenty of sockets—electrical equipment and visual aids are becoming more suitable for shops and will be used increasingly in the future. With the recent increase in regulations and related penalties regarding electrical and engineering installations (ventilating, heating and so on) it is wise to use reputable contractors at all times. Professional advice on the lighting levels for particular trades is readily available from the advisory services of the major lighting companies and Electricity Boards.

Heating and ventilation

Your customers and staff should be comfortable in your shop all year round. If possible, install heating which will provide sufficient all-round warmth during the cold months yet will convert to ventilation to keep the shop cool in summer. Many larger modern shops are fitted with sophisticated ducted heating and ventilation systems but these are often expensive to install and run. Smaller shops may use convector heaters and in these, and in larger stores, the use of warm air curtains at entrances keeps in much of the internal heat. Also for localised heating, overhead radiant or infra-red heaters can be useful. Night storage heaters may be suitable for many types of business. The high cost of energy (as with lighting) makes it important to seek professional advice as to the best system for your shop. Remember that low capital cost heaters may be energy inefficient, while more expensive systems can help conserve energy by their design and the use of thermostatic controls. Also, it is possible to conserve energy by the use of insulation materials.

Ceilings

A common ceiling material is plastic tiling. Sometimes this is mounted on a frame to provide a false ceiling upon which light fittings such as fluorescent tubes or spotlight tracks are mounted. The ceiling colour should complement that of the whole shop and thus, along with the materials used, will determine the amount of light absorbency/reflection. Lighting experts should be consulted on this latter point. Taking up the idea in the previous section, the ceiling should be constructed of well insulated materials because much of the ambient heat in the shop will otherwise disappear through it.

Fittings

The type of fittings you use in your shop will depend on the type of goods you sell, the level of service you offer and the sort of image you wish to present. Merchandise is usually displayed on wall fixtures or in free-standing or island units. The object of shopfittings is to display stock efficiently and attractively in order to enhance sales, so it is often money well spent. The keynote of modern retailing is flexibility, in line with the need to alter displays for seasonal requirements, to accommodate new lines and so forth. As a result, many shopfittings are now designed on a modular basis which means that they are manufactured in standard sections so that they can be changed around easily. It is not possible to deal exhaustively with the many kinds of fittings made for different trades and a retailer should seek the advice of a shopfitter. Shopfitters normally have catalogues illustrating all their standard units with measurements, materials used and so on. We shall therefore briefly discuss only the two basic kinds of fitting previously mentioned.

Wall units. Shelves should be flexible for various sizes of merchandise and should be adjustable so that sufficient space is left to allow easy selection. In most wall units the depth—front to back—increases in the lower shelves to feature the bulkier items. Make sure that the top shelf allows customers to see and select products easily, especially in self-service shops. In certain trades back lighting of shelving is very effective in showing off products to best effect.

Island units. If adequate floor space is available, free-standing units provide a useful method of displaying products. They should be shelved on both sides and both back and front. This is particularly true of self-service outlets. Hanging rails either in straight or circular ('spinner') stands are designed to display a large number of goods that stack flat. These are particularly useful in the fashion and allied trades. Other free-standing items include refrigerated units and cool counters for frozen foods and provisions and these should be maintained at recommended temperatures.

'Dump bins' are used very often for special promotions. Properly used they attract attention and promote sales because they make the line easy to pick up without the fear of disturbing a rear display and also project a 'bargain' image. Many manufacturers provide such free-standing units but they should only be accepted if they can provide a worth-while return and do not detract too much from the overall shop image. Remember that whatever fittings you use they should not create blind spots where customers cannot be seen because this will encourage pilferage. Again, customer circulation should not be hampered by too many of these units. Two people should be able to pass in comfort between them and so an aisle of at least 4 feet is required.

Another type of free-standing unit is, of course, the counter. Some trades still require this—for instance, the newsagent and the jeweller. The counter can also be used for display, either on the 'bed' or top, or the front (which must, of course, be glassed). The modern variant of the counter is the check-out, used in self-service outlets. These are available from simple L-shaped units to sophisticated affairs with a moving belt to speed up customer flow. Generally speaking, they should be as small as conveniently possible and yet allow the operator to sit on a stool and have room to work in comfort. The check-out can also provide a useful display point for 'impulse' lines like confectionery. The idea of the check-out (or cash point) is to speed up customer service, so do not overload it with merchandise!

Whether you run a self-service or a counter-service shop, you will need a cash register. This machine is an essential part of modern retailing because it not only keeps cash secure but also accounts for it. It adds up a customer's purchases and often computes the change (this is vital if we are to believe the allegation that arithmetic is not a strong point in school leavers!). The cash register can also be used for stock-keeping and sales analysis. Many of these machines are completely electronic and may be too expensive for some retailers. A few still keep their money in a cash drawer which provides no security and lacks a visual and formal record of sales to the customer. It is well worth while contacting some of the major cash register manufacturers for advice on these topics. Chapter 11 discusses the use of the cash register in more detail.

Shop layout

Now we have discussed the design and fittings of the 'box' let us turn to the actual layout. Space in a shop is used for four different purposes:

1. *Circulation.* Customers must have an area to walk round while inspecting goods.
2. *Display.* Merchandise, as we have seen, is shown either in wall fittings or in free-standing fittings.
3. *Selling.* In full personal-service shops, space is taken up by counters while the equivalent area in the self-service store is the check-out (or the cash-and-wrap or cash point).
4. *Ancillary.* These areas include stock-room, food preparation areas (if required), staff rest-rooms, offices and so on.

It is important to balance out the use of space, taking into account the considerations given above. Generally speaking, the amount of space you need to devote to your customers depends on your trade, the lines you are selling and the type of service you offer, but every retailer knows that one of the major problems is lack of space. The problem is how to use the existing space to make as much money as possible. Obviously you should give as much space as is feasible to goods on display and control the space for customers and for serving customers. We discuss the shop display below. Returning to the all-important customer it may be worth while asking yourself a few basic questions to see whether you have the right balance as far as customers are concerned:

1. Do my customers want to browse over any of the lines I sell? Will I benefit if I give them more opportunities to do so?
2. Are my products the type that require lengthy discussions with my customers before a sale is made?
3. Will I benefit if I provide chairs and a table for such discussions?
4. Does my shop become congested during peak shopping hours? Do I lose business because of this?
5. Would an increase in customer space help to solve this problem?
6. Are there any parts of my shop at present inaccessible to my customers, which it would benefit me to make accessible to them?
7. Are my competitors providing better customer facilities than I am? Do they gain business because of this?

If the answer to most of these questions is 'yes', you should consider giving more space to your customers. Alternatively, if you have answered mostly 'no', perhaps you now feel you are being over-generous to your customers and have space available to sell additional lines. Different retail trades adopt quite different approaches to layout. A typical hardware outlet will place high demand lines such as nails and screws at the back of the shop so that customers are forced past other high-profit impulse buying lines such as kitchen utensils and gifts. In CTNs (confectioner-tobacconist-newsagent shops), newspapers, confectionery and cigarettes are often located near the door because their sales peak in the morning and evening; customers shopping only for these items can be served quickly. Rear space is used for 'browsing' lines like greetings cards and records. Footwear shops, where most of the stock is in the window or round the walls, allow a large part of the space to customers, chairs and so on. Shops which sell large consumer durables, such as major domestic appliances and furniture, display much of their stock so that it is free-standing. Therefore the customer circulation area is the same as the display area.

In such trades as hardware, electrical and babywear, stock can be divided into a number of sections which form mini-departments of the shop. For example, in hardware shops such sections could be: gardening, home decoration and kitchen ware. In electrical retailing, the convention is to split the shop into 'brown' (TV/audio) and 'white' (major domestic appliances) and then to subdivide the sections further into, say, home laundry, refrigeration, large/portable TVs and so on. This logical approach helps customers and staff to find sections quickly.

Shop display

The last section gave some pointers on the general layout of a shop. Shop display is much more involved with the details of how the merchandise should be presented for maximum impact. There is an important distinction to be made here between counter and self-service shops. We have already seen that some trades such as jewellery and delicatessen need much more personal service. The customer has to enquire first of the counter assistant. In self-service, customers pick up the item (which is often pre-packaged) and take it to a check-out or cash point. Modern retailing methods suggest that it is better, as far as possible, to provide open displays which encourage customers to self-select. These methods reduce the physical and psychological barriers between the customer and the goods. Part of the attraction of self-service layout is the accessibility of the merchandise; the important transfer of ownership (physically and psychologically) is partly achieved by the open display. After all, the aspect of the retailing exercise is to sell the goods although they may be more open to pilferage and this is discussed in Chapter 11. Clearly it is impossible to convert all shops to self-service and this chapter discusses what can be done in counter-service as well as in self-service shops.

You will see from this that the term 'display' has a dimension other than visibility. We now discuss display in terms of the window and the customer area.

The window

This part of the shop is likely to be the first to attract the customer and is the first stage of enticing him or her into the interior. The traditional purposes of the window are:

1. To show a representative sample of merchandise sold in the shop.
2. To display promoted or seasonal lines.
3. To do both (1) and (2).

Purposes 2 and 3 provide an opportunity to change the window—an action too often neglected.

Most supermarkets and many self-service shops have dispensed with normal window displays and use the window to display the entire shop and its contents. Trades selling small items such as jewellery, or clothing and footwear shops, still rely on window displays, usually set off against a window back.

The basic principles of window display are similar to those for in-store display:

(a) Like products should be grouped together in the window; for example, radios, engagement rings.
(b) Featured or promoted lines should be placed in a prominent position in the windows and just below average eye-level.
(c) Window display height in a backless window should be between average waist and shoulder level so that customers look into the shop. Tall products like upright freezers should be displayed to the sides.
(d) Window displays should not be too deep. This will enable window-shoppers to see all the goods in the window clearly and, in the case of a backless window, to see into the shop.
(e) Where window space allows, mass or block displays of certain individual stock items such as promoted lines are valuable interest catchers.
(f) As many products as possible in the window should be ticketed and the price tickets should be in scale with the product.
(g) If windows are to be used as part of a positive effort to entice customers into the shop, displays should be changed regularly to keep up customers' interest. This has the added advantage of rotating window stock that might otherwise become faded, but staff should not make a habit of selling stock from the window display.
(h) Colour and movement are important in attracting attention. Boutiques, for instance, produce colourful displays using co-ordinated garments. Manufacturers' electrically driven turntables, which hold stock, are sometimes also useful.
(i) All stock and window fittings, such as shelving, should be clean; for example, bits of cotton left on men's suits in a window look particularly awful.
(j) Windows should be well lit, particularly for evening window shopping. Time clocks can be used to switch off lights in the window.

Window displays can be inspected before the shop opens and after it closes and, unlike press advertising, actual merchandise is used. Doors should be kept open as much as possible to encourage shoppers to walk in freely (the use of warm air curtains is mentioned on page 82). To summarise the advantages of window display changes:

1. Changing the display creates a lively enterprising image suggesting a shop where new things are happening and where new products may be found. Even if it is impossible to change the whole window often, the objects at the front should be changed frequently.
2. The shopkeeper is able to take advantage of special occasions such as Easter and St Valentine's Day and plan his display around them.
3. Customers are more likely to stop and look in if they become aware that there may be something new to see in the window.
4. In the case of shops such as boutiques, changes suggest that the previous clothes have been sold and that business is good; having the same suit or dress in the window for a fairly long time would suggest the reverse.
5. Some articles fade after a short time in the window.

In-store display

Once past the window line the customer is usually in the shop and the effect of good display continues to be important in catching his or her eye. Clever in-store display can be summed up in three words: logic, eye-appeal and accessibility.

Like products should be grouped together in displays, for example spin and tumble driers, sunglasses, large soft toys, cough mixture. The whole shop should be arranged as logically as possible in merchandise groupings. You will notice that most supermarkets run their merchandise logically within the store. For example, breakfast goods such as cereals and orange juice may be positioned adjacent to each other. Very importantly, products should be displayed in proportion to their sales and stock run. This is because display space is scarce in most retail outlets and modern merchandising methods demand that this space be used most profitably.

Eye-appeal of merchandise is improved by mass or block displays of identical items. A dump display of canned goods or a block display of boxed electrical toasters is almost essential, particularly when they are being promoted. Displays should not be too tidy and symmetrical because a certain amount of planned disarrangement can encourage the customer to buy. Point-of-sale material will often help increase sales but make sure that there is not an excess of suppliers' messages. This type of promotional material tends to creep over stock and windows, obscuring the real message of the product. Try, generally, to avoid clutter and the 'bazaar effect'. Stock should be regularly cleaned and dusted along with the shop, its frontage and fittings from the window line to the rear of the sales area. Damaged goods should never be on normal display but may be sold off at a discount in a 'bargain corner'. Displays of any product should be built so that they remain steady. Breakages cost money.

Merchandise should be as accessible as possible, depending on the type of goods sold, kind of service offered and so on. In some trades, such as toy and electrical shops, appropriate products should be working and demonstrable.

All lines carried in the shop should be on display (not just in stock) and correctly ticketed as necessary. Make sure, however, that the products you feature have sufficient back-stock; otherwise they should be sold as the off licence does its 'bin ends', that is, discounted and promoted as ends-of-lines. Best-selling lines on wall fittings should be displayed just at eye-level, medium sellers nearer the bottom and slower lines at the top. This is how the human eye travels over stock. By the same token, block displays of similar items should be displayed horizontally, not vertically. Obviously the size of the products will modify this approach, as described on page 83 on fittings. If you use free-standing or island fittings, the number one best seller in a range (preferably in a block display taking the whole position) should be on the front end nearest the door. The second best position is the back end shelving and the centre of both sides is a third equal best position. Check this in a Marks & Spencer store.

In the larger shop, signing is important. Make sure that any signs you put up to show where a section is are clear and visible to customers.

To summarise the objectives of window and in-store display:

1. To interest customers in merchandise and to draw them into the shop to enquire further.
2. In particular, to focus customers' interest on fast sellers and/or those products which are currently being promoted (for example, new lines).
3. To make it as easy as possible for customers to find and examine the goods they want.
4. To make it as easy as possible for sales assistants to find, demonstrate and sell the products.
5. To improve the image of the shop.

Chapter 11

Shop Operations

Your shop should be run as efficiently as possible for maximum success. This means that standards have to be set and procedures worked out for dealing with problems. Standards are applied to such areas as cleanliness, safety of staff and customers, maintenance of fittings and so on as well as to stock levels, security and credit control. Procedures are needed to deal with customers' complaints, customers caught shoplifting, accidents, breakdown of equipment and so forth.

This chapter deals with five main areas of shop operation: control of the physical environment, customer complaints, safety, security and cash control (stock control is covered in Chapter 8).

Shop environment

By this we mean the use of the shop premises and its fixtures and fittings.

Building fabric

The exterior of the building and the shop interior itself will need proper care and maintenance with special regard to the lease and any obligations agreed in it. Certainly if you are the freeholder, you will want to keep the property sound, not only as an operating asset but also as a capital investment with a resale value.

Heating

We previously mentioned that fittings should be purchased not only with their initial costs in mind, but also with regard to their operating costs. Heating equipment comes very much into this category because of the cost of energy. Thermostatic controls can be very useful in cutting heating costs, along with initial investment in good wall/ceiling insulating materials. Remember, however, that by cutting down too much on heating you can drive customers away. Make sure that you check heating apparatus regularly, particularly if it is run on paraffin. Safety is vital, especially from the point of view of fires.

Don't forget also to check visible wires and plugs in an electrical system (your property survey should have told you if you needed a complete rewiring of the premises).

Ventilation

A well-ventilated but draught-free shop is something that customers appreciate, especially in the food trades. The maintenance of clean air within the shop can be substantially affected by the heating and lighting levels, all of which are controlled by special legislation.

Lighting

As with heating, the initial choice of equipment can markedly influence the running costs. Points to note include the obvious one that natural lighting should be used as far as possible. When lights are used, see that the diffusers over fluorescent tubes are clean and that spare tubes and spotlight bulbs are kept handy. Time switches on window lights can save expense. In summer when the ambient heat builds up in the shop, some 'starters' can be removed from fluorescent tubes to reduce it.

Cleanliness

We have stressed elsewhere that the shop and its contents should be clean at all times from the window-line right to the end of the loading area at the back. Cleaning can be done by you or your staff at slack periods of the day. Depending on the floor area of the shop, you may need a heavy duty vacuum cleaner or polisher. Most shopping centres have several professional window-cleaners who tout for work as soon as a shop starts fitting out ready for the opening. Whether you or a window-cleaner make the windows sparkle is probably immaterial. But, as the 'eyes' of the shop, they must.

Fittings and equipment

You should see that all fittings, equipment, machinery and so on are maintained to a standard which contributes to the shop's sales success, but also keeps accidents to the minimum. One piece of equipment which can be expensive to run is the in-shop telephone, particularly if you employ staff. Unauthorised personal telephone calls can cost a lot and although these can be monitored in the budget, it may be useful to have a lock put on the instrument or even a coin-operated telephone installed. In a food shop, cool counter and refrigerated fitting temperatures should be monitored regularly to prevent either food spoilage or excessive electricity waste. Cutting and packaging equipment should be checked for safety on a regular basis.

Hygiene
In food shops particularly, good standards of hygiene should be maintained, not only because a lack of hygiene may drive customers away but because of the legislation covering it. Cleanliness of premises, fixtures, equipment and utensils has already been mentioned. In addition, staff in food shops must ensure that their hands are clean, and that they do not smoke, spit or sneeze over products, especially food. Cuts should be covered with a waterproof dressing. If any member of staff is suffering from an infection he or she should stay at home. Staff should wash their hands thoroughly after using the toilet. Personal clothing, overalls and uniforms should be kept clean. A special section for outdoor clothes must be provided.

The environmental health inspector can check a retailer's premises at any time to see that the Food Hygiene (General) Regulations 1970 and the Offices, Shops and Railway Premises Act 1963 are being observed. Failure to observe any of the rules can result in fines of up to £100 for each breach of the regulations, an order to clean things up or even to close down a business and the issue of a condemnation notice, for example for the disposal of food considered unfit for human consumption, by the inspector.

Customer complaints

Customers who complain to you are usually complaining about either the service or the merchandise. Complaints in the former category could be about long waits at check-outs or counters, staff rudeness or delivery delays. Merchandise complaints could concern their unsuitability or their condition. There is an old saying, 'The customer is always right.' Most complaints are genuine in reality and/or in the mind of the customer. The fact that the customer is irritated means that you'll have to respond in some way. Remember the customer is the most important person in your shop; it behoves you to try to solve the problem as quickly as possible to ensure that the customer does not leave the shop unsatisfied. First, try to get a clear picture of the complaint; by acting attentively, sympathetically and patiently you can help to calm the customer down and this process can be helped by the customer offering an explanation of the circumstances. Then it's your turn to explain, briefly, how the situation came about; the customer is not interested in the detailed reasons but only in what you intend to do about the problem.

Lastly, any action you take should be prompt. If the complaint is about merchandise you can offer a refund, a credit note or an exchange. You have to comply with the Sale of Goods Act 1893 and the Supply of Goods (Implied Terms) Act 1973. The second Act amended the first and states that goods must be of 'merchantable quality', they must be as described and must be fit for the purpose for which they are intended. Many customers know their rights today and will demand a refund. If you fail to satisfy the customer you may have lost him (or her) forever and ruined your shop's reputation with the customer and even with their family, friends and acquaintances. Remember, too, that if the customer is not right it can be useful to offer a 'goodwill' refund or exchange. The faulty goods should be put on one side for repair or return to the manufacturer. Make sure that the replacement is not faulty as well. If the complaint is about service, try to assure the customer that you genuinely regret the occurrence and that you and your staff will do all they can to make sure that it doesn't happen again. Of course, prevention is better than cure. A checklist to help:

1. Make sure that staff are well armed with product knowledge.
2. Make sure that package labels, instructions, size ticketing and so on of goods are complete and correct.
3. Make sure that staff are aware of the need to act courteously to customers at all times.
4. Make sure that goods are checked and that faulty or damaged goods are removed before they go on sale.
5. Make sure that written complaints are treated as seriously as verbal ones and dealt with promptly.
6. Check the shop floor regularly for long check-out queues, obstacles in aisles and so forth.

A few complaints will clearly be unjustified in the sense that the customer may be attempting to trick you into an exchange. In one case a few years ago a gang stole merchandise from one branch of a big chain store and asked for refunds on it in another branch. In this case the police were called in, but normally an unjustified complaint should be met with a firm refusal even if the customer argues. Giving way after a heated argument results in a loss without a corresponding increase in goodwill.

Safety

Under the 1974 Health and Safety at Work Act, standards for both customer and staff safety are laid down. The law for shops was originally drawn up under the Offices, Shops and Railway Premises Act, 1963. If customers are involved in accidents you and your staff should be helpful but non-committal, remembering that you may be at the start of an insurance claim against you. You should, of course, take out a policy for such happenings and your insurance broker will help here.

Security

Pilferage is the theft of cash or stock and makes up most of the unknown 'shrinkage' or difference between the estimated and the actual values of stock. Losses in this area are of two kinds: shoplifting and staff pilferage. The usual rate found in retailing organisations is between ½ and 1½ per cent of total sales. Not all of this shrinkage is deliberate, however, with about 10 per cent of it being due to inadvertent undercharging or the giving of too much change. As a whole pilferage is becoming a serious problem to retailers. Latest estimates reveal that well over £1 billion are lost in Britain every year from this cause and retailers are so concerned that the industry has set up the Association for the Prevention of Theft in Shops.

Shoplifting

This is the work of members of the public and is estimated to make up 30 per cent of unknown shrinkage (that is stock losses which cannot easily be traced to a known source, unlike breakages or stock deterioration). There are a number of methods of combatting shoplifting, including the following:

1. *Notices.* Prominently displayed notices warning people against shoplifting are a cheap and simple deterrent but whether they do much good is arguable. Big multiple chains state boldly on their notices 'Thieves will be prosecuted' or words to that effect. (Actual prosecution and its problems are discussed on page 97.)
2. *Store detectives.* These are more likely to be used in the larger store because they tend to be expensive. On the other hand, their success rate in apprehending thieves is reckoned to be good. A notice stating 'Store detectives are operating in this shop' could also help deter shoplifters. Most store detectives are women and they

can either be employed directly by the shopkeeper for peak trading periods or hired from a security organisation. (Names and addresses of some of these can be found in Yellow Pages.)

3. *Electronic systems.* There are a number of proprietary brands of system on sale, all of them with tags which are removed at the point of sale. Most potential shoplifters do not notice the sensitised tags which set off alarm bells at the entrance to the shop if taken through a photo-electric curtain. These systems, although expensive, are said to be beneficial, even reducing staff thefts of stock. The tags can also be used for stock control.
4. *Closed circuit television.* Video cameras, which are mounted in the store, transmit to monitor screens either in the sales area or the manager's office. This is an expensive system, normally used only in large department stores, petrol stations and so forth.
5. *Security mirrors.* These are round, convex mirrors available in various diameters. They are relatively cheap and therefore very suitable for smaller retailers. Positioned in blind spots, they act as a deterrent to shoplifting. One-way mirrors can also be fitted in the wall of the office if it overlooks the shop.
6. *Chains and loop alarms.* Popular in electrical goods shops for smaller audio, kitchen and personal care items, the simple chains are locked around a number of items, while allowing them to be examined individually. Loop alarms are similarly locked and, if broken, send out a high-pitched buzz.
7. *Fitting-room tags.* The fitting room in the clothing store is a favourite place for shoplifters to operate and customers are given hanger tags for each item taken in (usually with a maximum of two items allowed at a time).

One criticism of self-service and self-selection retail shops with their open displays is that they increase the risk of shoplifting. To help reduce these risks staff should be encouraged to be alert to suspicious movements. Anyone acting suspiciously should be approached with an offer of, 'Can I help you?' (one of the few occasions when this question should be used in a shop). Dark corners should be lit and mirrors installed in these areas. Small items such as pocket calculators and electric shavers should be displayed in glass-topped lockable show cases. Goods should be wrapped in close-fitting bags at the cash point so that further items cannot easily be pushed in. Large expensive items of stock should be displayed away from main doors and exit points. Cash registers should be kept locked and, as far as possible, out of the main customer flows (it has been known for cash registers near shop doors to be picked up and taken away by thieves).

If suspected shoplifters are stopped *in the shop* it is usual to give them the opportunity to pay by asking them if there is anything they wish to pay for. If they decline it is essential to wait until they have stepped out of the shop before asking them to return so that a check can be made on their purchases. A person can be arrested without warrant if he or she is seen stealing, or if a theft has occurred and there are 'reasonable grounds' for suspicion of that person. The police can be called and a witness to the incident should be present. All this should be done as quickly as possible, but it is vital that staff involved work to a pre-arranged system of apprehension. Most big retailers now make it a policy to prosecute shoplifters but this is a time-consuming process which will involve the presence of witnesses in court. For the smaller retailer with limited resources, the costs of prosecution may, regrettably, seem to outweigh the benefits. The same arguments can also be used for staff prosecutions for pilferage.

Staff pilferage

An estimated 60 per cent of unknown shrinkage is caused by direct staff thefts of stock or cash and collusion with delivery drivers, sales people and customers. One of the worst places for this kind of theft is the back door or goods reception point where security is often lax. Another popular area for staff pilferage is the stock-room. Staff should be made fully aware of the problems here and the consequences of dishonesty. Of course, staff pilferage is not necessarily going to occur, anyway, even if staff are employed, particularly if stringent recruitment and selection techniques are used. However, it is useful to remember that a number of things can be done to obviate these problems. A special staff area should be set aside where clothing and bags can be left during the day. A useful clause in a letter of appointment is one allowing spot searches of clothing and hand luggage. Valuable back stocks like cigarettes and watches can be placed in a safe, cage or specially secure area. Stocks generally should be kept in sealed outer packs; this not only minimises staff pilferage but also helps stocktaking. Strict cash till procedures, with occasional spot checks (matching sales read-out with the money actually in the till drawer), staff purchase, refund and exchange systems should be set up and implemented.

Errors

About 10 per cent of unknown shrinkage is due to incorrect change giving or undercharging. The section below on cash sales covers some of the points which staff have to note in this area. Suffice it to say that change should be *counted* out into customers' hands and not, as so often happens, given by the handful. Make sure that sales assistants use their cash register properly by reading off the price of each item before keying into the register and then pressing the total button; in most modern cash registers the amount tendered by the customer has to be keyed in too, and the balance (ie the change) is shown on the visual display as a check for both the assistant and the customer. Just think: how many customers complain that they have received too much change, rather than too little?

Shopbreaking

Fortunately, break-ins from outside the shop are much rarer than customer/staff pilferage, particularly as the loss is likely to be much greater. This type of theft is, of course, 'known' shrinkage and amounts stolen can be checked after the event, particularly if stock records are up to date.

Points to note here are:

1. A strict locking-up procedure should be followed each night and in reverse in the morning.
2. There should be secure locks on doors and windows at the front, side and rear, and on the roof.
3. Grille and other types of alarm should be set at a low sensitivity because they are liable to be disturbed by heavy traffic. Over 90 per cent of alarm calls in Britain are false due to incorrect setting.
4. Duplicate sets of keys should be held by some responsible person and/or at the local police station.
5. A security light should be left on at night. This is usually placed at the rear of the sales area.
6. A full audit of stock should be made as soon as possible after a break-in. Local valuers may be called in and their independent judgement is useful when the loss adjusters and insurance people move in.

Cash sales

Purchases are normally paid for either in cash, which includes cheque and credit card transactions, or on credit. Most retail sales are paid for in cash. Being in a cash business has many advantages. You do not have to pay your suppliers for maybe 30 days and can put the money into, say, a building society account until you need to make out your payment cheques. Alternatively, you can re-invest it immediately in stock, particularly if you can resell the stock quickly (in fact you can make a higher return on your money this way). You can also use it for paying wages or overheads such as electricity and telephone bills. The money should *not* be treated as drawings or used for unnecessary investment. One retailer was so overcome by his first week's takings of £1000 that he blew it all on a new central heating system, forgetting that he had to pay his suppliers and overheads out of this money.

The most usual method for the small retailer is the cash register system. The register can be mounted on counters, on checkouts, or at cash-and-wrap points, depending on the total selling system adopted. The cash register system means that the sales assistant takes the cash and completes the transaction personally. The cash register (or till as it is popularly called) is a very flexible tool because it can be moved around. For modern electric tills, electric points are, of course, required. The register is very useful in a high-volume, low-unit sale situation as in food shops. The till has many advantages, quite apart from the security aspect. Some small shops still use just a cash box or cash drawer where there is no direct record linking the goods sold and the money in the drawer. Information which can be got from a typical cash register includes:

1. Individual amounts for each separate item sold
2. Total value of each purchase
3. Discounts
4. Sub-total of sales at any time
5. Section or product range sales sub-totals
6. Number of customers and transactions.

Such information is essential for the proper control of the business over time. Detailed trends in sales can be spotted fairly quickly. This is another advantage of the retail shop—it is a 'here and now' situation and the cash register can help a lot in its successful running. Much of the information listed above can be printed on the tally roll, which can also be written on. At the beginning of each day's trading, a quantity of small change (the float) should be put in the till drawer to start the assistant building up change during the day. At the end of the day, registers are cashed-up, ie the cash should be counted and noted down, with the float figure deducted. This figure should be compared with the amount shown on the tally roll when the appropriate key is pressed. Takings should then be banked, minus float, using bank night safe wallets.

We have previously referred to the problems of change-giving which can lead to losses. When notes are tendered, they should be put on the 'slab' (the flat surface just under the keyboard), or stuck into a bulldog clip provided on the register itself, or corroborated with another assistant. With the growing use of higher denomination notes this simple procedure can avoid the arguments over the value of notes which can occur between sales staff and customers. After this, the amount is registered so that the correct signal is shown to the customer in the register window (this should never be obscured). The change is counted from the amount in the till window to the cash on the slab (subtracting), making up the difference between the two amounts. Some electronic point-of-sale terminals (the fashionable new name for the till) will show the relevant figures on their visual displays. The money on the slab or in the clip is then put in the till cash drawer and the change counted out into the customer's hand.

Cheques and forgeries

With the growing use of cheques, a number of things should be looked at when they are presented. The date should be correct and the cheque should be made out to the retailer. The amount in words and figures should tally, and it should be signed. It is usual for customers to be asked to back the cheque with a cheque card. This card should be current and you should write its number yourself on the backs of cheques up to £50. Above this figure the bank will not necessarily honour the cheque. There is really no need for customers to be asked to write their names and addresses on the back of a cheque (or in petrol stations their car registration numbers!) if all these procedures are followed. Remember, however, that more and more cheque books and cheque cards are being stolen or forged. The banks have produced the holographic cheque card to help prevent forgery and the use of cheques is diminishing with increased use of credit cards, Switch and Connect.

Normally if a retailer follows the procedures laid down by the banks and described briefly above, a 'bouncing' cheque will be fielded by the banking system itself.

Be wary of forged notes. There are some very convincing examples in circulation of the 'old' £20 note, complete with metal strip and watermark. However, in both respects they differ from the legal version and look rather drab.

Credit sales

Selling on credit means giving customers time to pay. By allowing credit you are effectively lending money to the customer. Normal short-term credit of up to one month does not attract a financial return in the way of interest charged. This kind of credit is extended as a means of creating more goodwill and, in a sense, it is a sales promotion. Any retailer of 'big ticket' items like major domestic appliances knows that customers cannot always find the total cash for payment immediately. Newsagents often allow credit on newspaper deliveries and the amount given will depend on the kind of area served and the newsagent's own judgement. If accounts of this kind are not paid promptly then the retailer has to provide the extra credit and this can reduce gross margins. Methods of credit used by smaller retailers include:

Payment out of income. Credit of this kind is popular for the purchase of goods such as clothing and toys for which hire purchase facilities are not normally available. Usually a down payment is made and the balance paid over a 6, 12 or 24 month period. An appropriate service charge is also made and this can be large enough to make a further contribution to profit.

Trading checks. Ownership of the goods passes legally to the purchaser and they cannot be recovered (unlike the situation with hire purchase). The trading check system is operated by finance companies such as the Provident Clothing and Supply Company Limited. They issue checks for the purchase of small items like clothing, repaid by weekly instalments collected by agents over a period of 20 weeks with a 5 per cent service charge. Vouchers for the purchase of consumer durables are also issued. In the case of Provident checks and vouchers, these are accepted by 60,000 retail outlets and some 15,000 agents visit customers in their homes each week to collect money and supply checks.

Hire purchase. This is the most popular method of purchasing durable goods on credit. In case of default on payment, the retailer has the right to repossess the goods under certain conditions; the goods are not sold outright, only hired to the customer, unlike the somewhat similar credit sale agreements where the goods become the property of the customer immediately. Normally the retailer seeks support from a finance house rather than supporting the loan himself. The retailer then collects payments and refunds the finance house.

Credit cards. The two best-known credit cards are, of course, Access and Barclaycard (Visa). The latter is provided by Barclays Bank, and Access by the other London clearing banks, together with the Royal Bank of Scotland. These organisations provide credit facilities to retailers who accept the cards. The retailer in the scheme allows the customer credit on purchases up to a particular limit. The bill is immediately presented by the shop owner to the bank who pays him the cash. For this the retailer pays approximately 2 per cent of the value of the sale as a service charge. The retailer also pays a sum to join the scheme. The problem here is that low margins, such as in bookselling, are reduced still further. This is why you may be better off not accepting them at all.

Club trading. This is not strictly credit selling in the normal sense because the retailer takes no risk. What happens is that a toyshop, for instance, encourages customers to pay a weekly sum for the article they wish to buy. Members of the club draw lots as to the order in which they are to receive the goods, the holder of number one receiving the goods after the first payment and the last member when making the last payment. If you offer credit as a retailer you are subject to the Consumer Credit Act 1974.

There is no doubt that credit systems can be advantageous to you in certain kinds of retailing, eg furnishings, domestic appliances, clothing and toys. Sales can be boosted and more higher value items purchased. Customers come into the shop more frequently to pay and, generally, goodwill is increased. On the other side, you may have to borrow additional capital to fund the debt and have to pay interest on it. Administratively, too, credit control can be time-consuming and costly. In some cases you may even have to face the possibility of losses from bad debts.

Really there is no point in offering credit in your shop unless it produces a sufficient increase in profits (not just turnover) to cover interest charges on borrowed capital, administration costs and bad debts. You have to ask yourself whether you could use the capital involved more profitably in other ways. If you do offer credit you have, of course, the right to refuse it: it is not the automatic right of every customer. This is where credit control comes in. Customers requesting credit facilities may be investigated before being allowed to enter into an agreement. An application form, usually supplied by the finance company if you are funding the debt from external sources, should be filled in by the potential borrower. By answering questions on income, home ownership status, use of bank account, employer and so on, the credit status of the customer can be established by the finance company or an external credit status agency. Reminders to slow payers may in this case be handled by the finance company. If you handle the credit yourself all aspects of credit vetting, administration and control must fall on you and your staff. If you *have* to offer credit make sure it is done systematically. Keep careful records and chase up promptly in cases of accounts falling in arrears. Try charging interest on these and see what happens, if anything!

Measuring performance

It was mentioned at the beginning of this chapter that you should set standards of performance in all sorts of matters. The sum total of all this should be the sales and profit performance of the shop itself. There are a number of key indicators here:

Sales per square foot (or metre). Let's say your sales area is 1000 square feet and that over the year your sales were £90,000. This means that your sales conversion factor is £90 for the year, ie £90,000/1,000. Now this figure on its own doesn't mean very much, but when you compare it with what was done last year, say, £75 per square foot, you can see that there has been a marked improvement in the use made of the space available during the year when you took out the old window beds. It is also useful to compare, if possible, with what other retailers achieve in the same trade as yours. Unfortunately retailers are generally a secretive breed and very few figures are published. A sophistication is to work out the gross profit per square foot.

Sales per linear foot (or metre). Many big stores measure their sales (and profits) in relation to the length of counter or shelf they carry in their stores. This gives a much better indication of the success of in-store display and merchandising in particular sections and brings out the existence of 'hot spots'—areas of high volume—and 'dead areas'. Much more time has to be spent on this kind of measurement, particularly when you are relating the shelf space allocated to one kind of product to the gross profit margin which the sales have earned. The theory is that you should try to allocate space to products in line with their individual sales or profits.

Sales per assistant. This is a key measurement in all kinds of financial analysis and is effectively a measure of labour productivity. You can also work out a net profit per assistant and this will help you to work out how much more you need to sell to pay for another staff member. For example, if you pay a part-timer £50 a week and your net margin is 5 per cent on sales of £250,000, ie £12,500, the part-timer will have to contribute another £50,000 a year in sales to pay his way. With part-timers make sure you measure on the basis of hours worked.

Sales per cash register. If a cash register serves a particular part of a shop then its recorded sales may give some idea of the success of that section. It was mentioned earlier that cash registers can be used to record detailed sales in particular products or sections of a shop. In a supermarket, by dividing the period's sales by the number of check-outs, the owner can find out whether he is 'under' or 'over-tilled' and make adjustments.

Cyclometers and sales cards. When new lines are being introduced it is useful to monitor their progress individually for a week or so by the use of cyclometers (clicking counters) or by using the 'five-bar gate' method of marking on a sales card. Marks & Spencer use both methods. One big drawback here is that staff may forget to mark in sales, particularly at busy times.

Rate of stockturn. Although this has already been discussed it is worth mentioning again in this context. There is proof of a strong connection between rate of stockturn and the size of net margins and therefore on return on capital employed. In food stores stockturn rates, which are calculated by dividing average stock at selling price into sales, may be as high as 25 times (four weeks' average stock). In non-foods, turns of 6 to 8 times would be considered acceptable.

Chapter 12

Improving Performance

It is one thing to open a shop and another to wait for customers to come in. The first day of opening is a thrilling and sometimes a frightening experience. You may stand and wait while customers float past your window, almost as though you and your shop were not there. Why don't they come in?

It may be simply that they haven't noticed your new shop, particularly if you have not given it that lick of paint or new fascia mentioned in Chapter 10. You may not have advertised or promoted the shop at all, relying on existing custom (if you have taken over a business) or on the associated sales which other shops around you provide by their presence and their customer generation.

The point is that some people within your catchment area, the area from which your shop and others around you draw their custom, may never enter your shop because they have found what they regard as the answer to their shopping problems in a more convenient location. Shoppers are conservative: once we've found what we want we are often loath to change. Something important must change for us in the shopping environment if we are to alter our habits. This is where marketing comes in. For the retailer the most important aspects of marketing are the produce range offered, the price level, location of the shop, and the promotions mounted to attract custom. We have already discussed the first three, which leaves promotion. Promotion is any direct method used to increase the sales level. Promotion is of four main kinds: advertising, publicity, sales promotion and personal selling (the last we dealt with in Chapter 9).

Advertising

The word advertising conjures up visions of dark-suited executives discussing creative and media strategies in plush offices in London's West End—and lots of expense. Advertising need not be costly for the retailer.

Advertising is of two kinds: tactical and strategic. This

means that the objectives of advertising can be different. Short-term or tactical advertising stimulates traffic building within days of the appearance of an advertisement, usually by means of a specific merchandise or promotional offer. Long-term or strategic advertising is aimed at building 'brand loyalty'. This means that the objective of the communication is to persuade an increasing number of customers in the shop's catchment area that the advertised store is the right choice for the classes of merchandise which are on sale. This builds up the repeat purchase situation so that shoppers become habitually committed to your shop and cannot think of a better alternative. This latter kind of advertising is most important in creating a long-term future for the shop by changing people's attitudes towards it.

The advertising media or channels through which a retailer can reach potential or existing customers are many. They vary both in effectiveness and in cost, although it is not necessarily true that the most expensive methods of advertising are necessarily the best for the small retailer. For example, television is prohibitively expensive and although many big multiple chains use it regularly, it is clearly not for small retailers.

Local radio

Local radio is becoming more popular with smaller retailers. This medium is much more cost-effective than TV. Details of costs, geographical coverage and audiences can be obtained from the radio station's marketing department. The station may also be happy to put you in touch with successful advertisers similar to yourself.

Local press

Local newspapers, including the many free newspapers, are often useful media for the retailer. Generally, retailers will take display advertising space rather than classified. The latter involves the two- or three-line advertisements found in columns headed 'Cars for sale' or 'Catering services'. Display advertising is cross-columnar and often involves the use of blocks for line drawings or photographs. Classified advertisements are used mainly when something specific is being sold whereas display advertising is more of the 'tactical' or 'strategic' types mentioned previously. Advertising is a constant reminder of the presence of the shop, and press adverts are particularly useful for informing customers of special promotions and so on. Single advertisements inserted at infrequent intervals are largely a waste of money. They do not breach the 'communication threshold' (as the jargon of advertisers has it). Advertising needs to be seen and remembered and that is why size—and repetition—are useful. Of course the bigger and more frequent the advertising is, the more expensive it becomes. But business people should not dwell exclusively on the costs of media but should consider the benefits as well. Again, the local newspaper office may be able to provide documented evidence of successful advertising in similar circumstances to your own. Their marketing department will also let you have costs, circulation and readership figures.

Cinema

Local cinema can offer good service to the local retailer. Recently there has been a trend towards increasing audience sizes because of better quality films. Audiences vary depending on the film being shown, although the majority are composed of young people. Certain times are often cheaper for pensioners. The local cinema manager should be able to give you details of rates, attendances, and forthcoming films.

Direct mail

Direct mail is the third most important medium in Britain and certainly the fastest growing today, although the amounts spent are still well below those on TV and print. Direct mail involves sending brochures or handbills either through the post or by hand through letterboxes. These mailshots can be designed and printed locally at reasonable expense and, if you have a list of existing customers, this will form a handy mailing list.

Posters

One of the distressing things about independent shop operation is the proliferation of 'home-made' posters in windows and in-store. Fortunately, many manufacturers supply their own posters to underpin promotions and so on. If you are mounting your own promotion, try to have the posters created professionally by a print shop, making sure that you order a design which will cause shoppers to pause as they pass the shop.

Publicity

Publicity can be defined as news about products or businesses appearing in the form of editorial material without cost to the sponsor. This means that the actual space in the newspaper or time on television or radio is 'free' and not paid for by the person or business benefiting. The value of publicity is that when it is part of the feature and news content of a paper or broadcast it is much more likely to be noticed and believed than if it is just a paid advertisement.

Examples of publicity include the use of sponsorship by sports shops. Here a cycle shop, for example, sponsors a skilful BMX bike rider by lending him equipment. When the boy wins a local race, the connection between the shop and the sports winner can be mentioned in the news coverage. A shop selling bridal wear in the West Country was able to receive mentions in local reports of the wedding, with the agreement of the couples involved. Such publicity must be done skilfully and you must remember that newspapers thrive on interesting news which will keep its readership happy.

A straight statement that your bridal shop has sold its two hundredth wedding dress is hardly newsworthy until it is linked with the speculation that the district is made up of reasonably well-heeled and mature families.

In a wider context it is good business to increase the amount of non-media publicity as well. If customers are satisfied with your shop and what it stocks then, invariably, it will be talked about. Personal recommendation is often worth more than advertising or publicity because it is offered, usually, in a quite impartial way. This can increase the credibility of your business markedly. The only problem is that this form of communication takes a long time to develop.

Sales promotion

Sales promotion is any non face-to-face activity concerned with the promotion of sales and usually excluding advertising and publicity. It is very important in retail marketing. The goals of sales promotion are:

1. *Stop and shop.* Customers passing the shop who have no intention of going in can be encouraged to enter by display features inside the shop or in the window.
2. *Shop and buy.* Having persuaded customers to enter the shop, you should now encourage them to buy by exhibiting the merchandise in such a way as to create a desire to purchase in the consumer's mind—perhaps an attractive display of Easter eggs.
3. *Buy bigger.* During the buying process sales promotion can help to persuade the customer to buy either a larger

quantity of the same goods or to buy other products in addition, eg by lowering the price of larger packs or offering joint promotions on, say, eggs and bacon.

4. *Repeat purchase.* The final aim is to persuade the customer to return again and again to your shop, trading on the goodwill and loyalty that has been instilled by previous purchases and service.

Suppliers' promotions

Manufacturers are the biggest source of promotions and there are 12 basic kinds:

1. *Price-off pack.* Here something like '10p off' is printed or branded on the pack.
2. *Gifts.* Often called 'premiums', these may be small plastic toys or badges either in or, occasionally, attached to the pack.
3. *Self-liquidating premiums.* The customer is offered a lower than normal price for a special product which accompanies the promoted merchandise; these special premiums are bought in bulk by the manufacturer and their bought-in costs are covered by the money paid for them by the customer who takes up the offer.
4. *Coupons.* Price-off coupons are printed on the packs or in newspapers and allow a reduction in the price of the next purchase of the brand. Manufacturers become very agitated when 'mal-redemption' occurs, ie the coupon is used to reduce the costs of goods other than the brand mentioned on the coupon.
5. *Buy one, get one free.* Usually the customer has to send pack tops to the manufacturer and it is somewhat similar to couponing.
6. *Multi-packs.* Two packs are attached together and sold for the price of one at the time of purchase. Occasionally a stretched version of the pack (30 per cent extra!) obviates the need for extra shelf space with the normal multi-pack.
7. *Competitions.* These are often printed on the packs or, as in the drinks trade, on a collar round the neck of the bottle.
8. *Cooperative promotions,* eg two or more branded products sharing and financing a joint in-store promotion such as garden peat and packet seeds.
9. *Sampling.* The giving away, often in the shop, of product

samples sometimes with a demonstrator present, eg Swiss cheese, Cyprus sherry.

10. *Bingo/games of chance,* eg the Shell 'Make Money' campaign. Although this particular game was not illegal because players did not have to purchase petrol, other similar games have been declared so.
11. *In-store salesgirls.* Variations on demonstrators are used, for example, in the electrical major domestic appliances or 'white goods' market. To work well there probably has to be a further inducement such as reduced prices.
12. *Personality promotions.* Some manufacturers have been using show-business personalities to promote their products but this can be expensive and produce over-exposure.

You may well see some ideas in the foregoing list which you can use in your shop. Be prepared for special selling times such as Mother's Day, summer holidays and return to school, Hallowe'en, skiing holidays, Christmas and the new year.

Many manufacturers produce sales material for placing near the products themselves. Examples of these are:

(a) *Special fittings,* such as paperback publishers' racks, dry-battery stands.
(b) *Showcards* designed to stand on or fit round the product as with washing machine 'crowns'.
(c) *Leaflets and product labels.*

Joint ventures

Collaboration with other shopkeepers can also bring cheap or even free publicity. A grocer might, for example, advertise that every twenty-fifth pack of a certain product line he wants to clear quickly has in it a voucher worth, say, £3 which can be used against purchases in a local electrical shop. The electrical retailer may be glad to contribute half the cost of the voucher in return for bringing extra customers into his shop.

At Christmas time the shops in some centres hire decorations and share the cost between them. This is a good example of a truly joint promotion, but such exercises cannot really succeed unless they have the support of all the retailers concerned.

Seasonal sales

Everybody buys wrongly sometimes. You may buy the wrong

merchandise which your customers fail to take up—for some reason which you should try to find out. Maybe you bought too much of a good thing and, faced with a high overstock, you quail. The answer may well be a sale. Seasonal sales are particularly useful in the textile trades but most trades, apart from those in food or in fmcg lines (marketing shorthand for 'fast moving consumer goods'), give you the opportunity to mark down discreetly a failed line on its shelf. Sales can be held twice yearly, as in the winter sale (just after Christmas) or more often in the summer sale. This ties in with the two-season textile trades where women's clothes ranges, for example, are changed over and non-sellers sold off.

This brings us to the 'mark-down'. A mark-down is a percentage cut in the original selling price of the product. Make sure that it is not more than the mark-up from the buying price, otherwise you have a 'loss leader' on your hands. This pricing method is sometimes used by grocery supermarkets to draw customers in because it involves the deep cut pricing of products whose prices are well known to the customer, such as tea, sugar, washing powder and other staple commodities. The idea is to project an atmosphere of low prices—not the sort of thing you necessarily want to do if you are running a boutique. Returning to sales, a good deal of merchandise is often bought in (particularly by department stores) to supplement genuine mark-downs. The bought-in lines are often seconds or slightly faulty goods sent out by the manufacturers without labels. Retailers may wish to investigate such lines and contacts should include conventional wholesalers, general merchants, importers and others.

Some perishable lines in food shops may be at the limit of their freshness date or shelf-life. Such products should be put together in a prominent place and marked for quick sale.

Checklist: how to increase sales

1. Ensure, by means of market research if necessary or possible, that you are selling what your customers want to buy. Be willing to try new products and change stocking policy when and if required.
2. Let the customers know what you are offering by as economic a method as possible. This could be by putting a notice in the shop window, handbills through customers' doors or by an advertisement in the local press. You may find that the cost of advertising at your

local cinema is quite reasonable. The best advertising of all is free advertising and this can sometimes be obtained by getting a mention in the editorial columns of the local paper. To achieve this, of course, you must have some new product to discuss or something of interest to say about your existing lines or the shop itself.

3. Take advantage of any special deals by manufacturers or suppliers. Some, for example, may supply catalogues of their products which can be stamped on the front with your shop's name and address. More useful is the custom of a manufacturer or supplier supplying a rack of goods which he is responsible for maintaining. Such racks may be seen in bookshops, for example. The shopkeeper pays the supplier a percentage on the goods sold but is saved the trouble of looking after that rack or shelf and may be able to stock more interesting goods—those which a large wholesaler would not carry.
4. Consider stocking products that are made locally, for example home-made quiches, pottery. Non food items may be stocked on a sale or return basis.
5. Relevant businesses may consider offering a hiring service for some of their goods, for example a dry cleaner's or electrical shop may offer a steam carpet/upholstery cleaner for hire.
6. It may be worthwhile to offer a delivery service even if you have to charge the customer for it.
7. Ensure that your staff are well trained and enthusiastic.

Chapter 13

Further Information

Gross profit margins for UK stores

Gross profit is expressed as a percentage of sales.

	Percentage
Total retail businesses	29.4
Food retailers	22.8
Large grocery retailers	21.9
Other grocery retailers	19.2
Dairymen	27.7
Butchers, poulterers	25.9
Fishmongers	26.7
Greengrocers, fruiterers	26.8
Bread and flour confectioners	47.2
Drink, confectionery and tobacco retailers	18.2
Retailers of confectionery, tobacco and newsagents	18.5
Off-licences	17.0
Clothing, footwear and leather goods retailers	43.4
Men's and boys' wear retailers	44.7
Women's, girls', children's and infants' wear retailers	45.1
General clothing businesses	40.5
Footwear retailers	43.0
Leather and travel goods retailers	38.7
Household goods retailers	34.1
Household textiles retailers	36.8
Carpet retailers	33.7
Furniture retailers	36.4
Electrical, gas and music goods retailers	31.8
Hardware, china and fancy goods retailers	37.2
Do-it-yourself retailers	33.5

	Percentage
Other non-food retailers	33.0
Chemists	25.6
Newsagents and stationers	37.1
Booksellers	40.1
Photographic goods retailers	22.6
Jewellers	43.2
Toys, hobby, cycle and sports goods retailers	32.0
Florists, nurserymen and seedsmen	40.0
Non-food retailers (others)	32.6
Mixed retail businesses	33.2
Large mixed businesses	30.6
Other mixed businesses	31.5
General mail order houses	46.3
Hire and repair businesses	69.8
Television hire businesses	68.9
Other hire or repair	74.5

Source: *Business Monitor* 1991

Useful addresses

Advisory, Conciliation and Arbitration Service (ACAS)
27 Wilton Street, London SW1X 7AZ; 071-210 3645 (and local offices)

Alliance of Small Firms and Self Employed People
33 The Green, Calne, Wiltshire SN11 8DJ; 0249 817003

Association for the Prevention of Theft in Shops
180 Wardour Street, London W1V 3AA; 071-505 1695

British Franchise Association (BFA)
Thames View, Newton Road, Henley-on-Thames, Oxon RG9 1HG; 0491 578049

Employment Department
Small Firms Service
Dial freefone 0800 222999 and ask for freefone Enterprise direct.

Charles Goad Ltd
8–12 Salisbury Square, Old Hatfield, Hertfordshire AL9 5BJ; 07072 71171

National Association of Shopkeepers
Lynch House, 91 Mansfield Road, Nottingham NG1 3FN; 0602 475046

National Chamber of Trade
Enterprise House, Henley-on-Thames, Oxon RG9 1TU; 0491 5766161

Rural Development Commission (formerly CoSIRA)
141 Castle Street, Salisbury, Wiltshire SP1 3TP; 0722 336255 (and local offices)

Small Business Bureau
32 Smith Square, London SW1P 3HH; 071-222 0330

The Unit for Retail Planning Information Ltd
7 Southern Court, South Street, Reading RG1 4QS; 0734 588181

Further reading

Some of the best known trade papers and magazines:

The Bookseller
British Baker
Cabinet Maker and Retail Furnisher
Carpet and Floor Coverings Review
Chemist and Druggist
Convenience Store
Co-operative News
DIY Week
DRI—The Fashion Business
Electrical and Radio Trading
Fashion Weekly
Fish Trader
Florists' News
Franchise World
Furnishing
The Grocer
Hardware Today
Health Retailer
Meat Trader
Meat Trades Journal
Men's Wear
Music Week
Off-licence News
Pet Business World
Photo and Electronics Marketing
Retail Confectioner Tobacconist
Retail Fruit Trade Review
Retail Jeweller
Retail Week
Retail Newsagent Tobacconist Confectioner
Shoe and Leather News
Sports Retailing

Supermarketing
Toy Trader

Business books

Baffled by Balance Sheets?, W L Johnson (Kogan Page)
BA Guide to Starting and Running a Bookshop, Malcolm Breckman (Booksellers Association)
Be Your Own Company Secretary, A J Scrine (Kogan Page)
Buying a Shop, 3rd edition, A St J Price (Kogan Page)
Croner's Reference Book for the Self Employed and Smaller Business (Croner Publications, Croner House, London Road, Kingston-upon-Thames, Surrey KT2 6SR)
Do Your Own Bookkeeping, Max Pullen (Kogan Page)
The Good Franchise Guide, Tony Attwood and Len Hough (Kogan Page)
How to Buy a Business, 2nd edition, Peter Farrell (Kogan Page)
How to Deal With Your Bank Manager, Geoffrey Sales (Kogan Page)
How to Prepare a Business Plan, Edward Blackwell (Kogan Page)
How to Promote Your Own Business, Jim Dudley (Kogan Page)
Importing for the Small Business, 2nd edition, Mag Morris (Kogan Page)
Law for the Small Business, 7th edition, Patricia Clayton (Kogan Page)
Management of Trade Credit, T G Hutson and J Butterworth (Gower Press)
Retail Management, Roger Cox and P Britten (Macdonald and Evans)
Running Your Own Hairdressing Salon, Christine Harvey and Helen Steadman (Kogan Page)
Starting a Successful Small Business, 2nd edition, M J Morris (Kogan Page)
Successful Marketing for the Small Business, 2nd edition, Dave Patten (Kogan Page)
Taking up a Franchise, 8th edition, Colin Barrow and Godfrey Golzen (Kogan Page)
Understand Your Accounts, 3rd edition, A St J Price (Kogan Page)

Index

add=address